THE STORY OF ART
~~WITHOUT MEN~~
KATY HESSEL
Illustrated by
PING ZHU

Katy Hessel is an art historian from London, UK. She is the author of three books, including the adult edition of *The Story of Art Without Men*, and *How To Live An Artful Life*. In 2015, she founded @thegreatwomenartists on Instagram, where she celebrates women artists on a daily basis, and hosts the podcast of the same name. She has interviewed hundreds of artists, curated exhibitions across the globe, lectured at The National Gallery and presented programmes for the BBC. A Visiting Fellow at the University of Cambridge, a Trustee at Charleston (the former home of the Bloomsbury Group) and a columnist for the *Guardian*, Katy also writes audio guides for museums all over the world – that are all free to listen to – called *Museums Without Men*.

THE STORY OF ART WITHOUT MEN

KATY HESSEL

Illustrated by
PING ZHU

PUFFIN

To Jesse, Phoebe, Thea and Cleo

PUFFIN BOOKS

UK | USA | Canada | Ireland | Australia
India | New Zealand | South Africa

Puffin Books is part of the Penguin Random House group of companies whose addresses can be found at global.penguinrandomhouse.com

www.penguin.co.uk   www.puffin.co.uk   www.ladybird.co.uk

First published 2026
001

Text copyright © Katy Hessel, 2026
Illustrations copyright © Ping Zhu 2026
The moral right of the author and illustrator has been asserted

Every effort has been made to trace copyright holders and to obtain their permission for the use of copyright material. The publisher apologizes for any errors or omissions and if notified of any corrections will make suitable acknowledgement in future reprints or editions of this book.

Penguin Random House values and supports copyright. Copyright fuels creativity, encourages diverse voices, promotes freedom of expression and supports a vibrant culture. Thank you for purchasing an authorized edition of this book and for respecting intellectual property laws by not reproducing, scanning or distributing any part of it by any means without permission. You are supporting authors and enabling Penguin Random House to continue to publish books for everyone. No part of this book may be used or reproduced in any manner for the purpose of training artificial intelligence technologies or systems. In accordance with Article 4(3) of the DSM Directive 2019/790, Penguin Random House expressly reserves this work from the text and data mining exception.

Text design by Sophie Gordon

Printed and bound in China

The authorized representative in the EEA is Penguin Random House Ireland, Morrison Chambers, 32 Nassau Street, Dublin D02 YH68

A CIP catalogue record for this book is available from the British Library

ISBN: 978–0–241–73819–1

All correspondence to:
Puffin Books
Penguin Random House Children's
One Embassy Gardens, 8 Viaduct Gardens, London SW11 7BW

Penguin Random House is committed to a sustainable future for our business, our readers and our planet. This book is made from Forest Stewardship Council® certified paper.

CONTENTS

10 — INTRODUCTION

18 — THE RENAISSANCE: PORTRAITURE AND STILL LIFE

26 — BAROQUE AND BOTANY

34 — BREAKING THE GLASS CEILING: NEOCLASSICISM

38 — SPOTLIGHT: NEEDLEWORK

40 — VICTORIAN BRITAIN: NEW PROGRESSIONS AND NEW INVENTIONS

48 — IMPRESSIONISM

54 — EXPRESS YOURSELF

62 — MACHINES AND THE FIRST WORLD WAR

68 — SURREALISM

74 — SPOTLIGHT: FRIDA KAHLO

76 — THE HARLEM RENAISSANCE

82 — NEW LANDSCAPES: BRAZIL AND THE UNITED STATES

88 — ABSTRACT EXPRESSIONISM

94 — A NEW TYPE OF ART: EXPERIMENTATION

100 — MINIMALISM

106 — POP ART

112 — BLACK POWER: THE CIVIL RIGHTS MOVEMENT

120 — TEXTILES: 1950S TO THE PRESENT DAY

126 — THE 1970S AND THE FEMINIST MOVEMENT

132 — THE 1980S

140 — BRITAIN IN THE 1990S

146 — FIRST NATIONS ART IN AUSTRALIA

152 — A NEW ART FOR A NEW MILLENNIUM

158 — ART FOR THE NEW WORLD

164 — CONCLUSION

TIMELINE OF MOVEMENTS

THE RENAISSANCE
c.1350–1600

BAROQUE
c.1600–1750

ART DURING THE FIRST WORLD WAR
c.1910–1920

SURREALISM
c.1920–1960

ABSTRACT EXPRESSIONISM
c.1945–1960

EXPERIMENTATION IN POST-WAR ART
c.1945–1955

PICTURES GENERATION
c.1975–1985

THE FEMINIST ART MOVEMENT
c.1970–1980

A NEW BRITISH ART
c.1990–2000

FIRST NATIONS ART IN AUSTRALIA
c.1980–now

MINIMALISM
c.1955–1970

POP ART
c.1955–1970

THE FIBRE ART
MOVEMENT
c.1960–1980

BLACK POWER:
THE CIVIL RIGHTS
MOVEMENT
c.1955–1970

ART IN THE
21ST CENTURY
2000s–now

WHAT IS
ART NOW?
2020s–now

INTRODUCTION

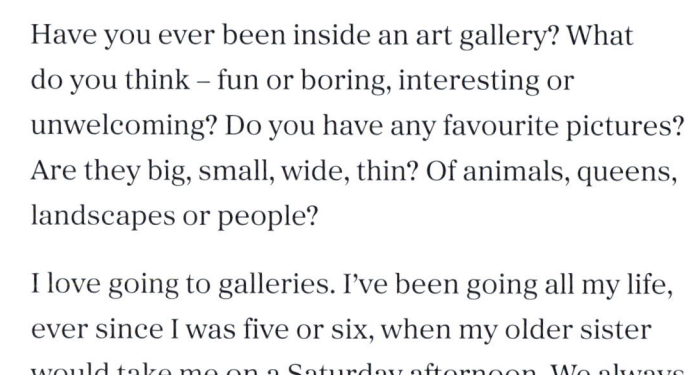

Have you ever been inside an art gallery? What do you think – fun or boring, interesting or unwelcoming? Do you have any favourite pictures? Are they big, small, wide, thin? Of animals, queens, landscapes or people?

I love going to galleries. I've been going all my life, ever since I was five or six, when my older sister would take me on a Saturday afternoon. We always brought our sketchbooks, and drew what we saw.

Sometimes, it's difficult to relate to the people in the pictures. They can be from 10, 50, 100 or even 500 years ago, living a life that is very different to both yours and mine. Yet we still write and talk about them, and go and visit them in galleries. So, **WHAT'S THE FUSS?**

ARTWORKS TELL THE HISTORY OF THE WORLD THROUGH THE PEOPLE WHO MADE THEM. They can tell us about what someone was interested in at a certain time, or how they felt. Through them, we can peer into the minds and lives of the people who came before us. Despite some art being thousands of years old, it can still tell an artist's story.

Art – like music, dance or writing – is a way of communicating about what's going on in the world, and a way to express yourself.

If you had some paints, pencils or clay, and were to use them to describe the way you feel or to show what's happening in your life, what would you make? Would you draw your cat? A family member? The view outside your window? The night's sky, a story you heard recently, or a memory?

Art (what we sometimes call **ARTWORKS** or **WORKS**) can tell a story of how we got to where we are now.

This is known as **ART HISTORY** (my favourite subject), which follows art through time. Art history is often made up of *movements*, which help describe a style used by artists working at one time, or who live in the same place.

If you've ever stepped inside an art gallery (and don't worry if you're yet to, I am hoping this book will be your inspiration to start!), you'll notice that rooms or sections are divided by styles or movements. For example, **IMPRESSIONISM** (which you'll learn about on page 48) is named because the artists were making an 'impression' (a fleeting glimpse, not a detailed picture) of something.

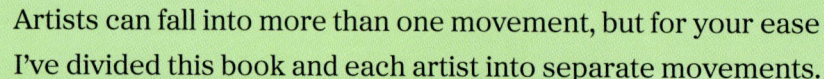

Artists can fall into more than one movement, but for your ease I've divided this book and each artist into separate movements.

Art historians like me create labels (such as names for movements in history) in order to understand the history of the world – and to help guide you, the reader. Without these categories, we'd have no structure. Imagine it a bit like a house. All your items and furniture are inside it, but without the bricks, the house will probably fall down. Art historians are like builders, creating a solid structure with bricks.

But when you think about what makes a house a home, it's not the bricks, but the people, memories and belongings that fill it. **AND THAT'S WHAT THIS BOOK IS REALLY ABOUT – THE INCREDIBLE ARTISTS, THEIR STORIES, THEIR LIVES AND THEIR WORK.**

HELLO, I'M KATY.

I'm an art historian and I'll be guiding you through this book. My job involves looking at pictures all day and writing about them. It's not bad! I've loved writing about art since I was a teenager. I'd write mini reviews in what I called my 'art diaries', where I'd jot down a few words about the pictures I'd seen. You should try it!

SOME TIPS FOR WRITING ABOUT ART

Ask yourself: How does that work make me feel? What hidden messages can I find in a painting or photograph? Where and when was the work made, and who made it? Your writing about art is no different from what I've done in this book, as an art historian.

BUT WHY IS THIS A HISTORY OF ART WITHOUT MEN?

At the grand old age of 21, I noticed something. I was visiting an art fair (like a big shop, where galleries sell pictures by artists). I looked around at the artworks, and realized not a single one was by a woman. I was shocked! Not only because of the lack of female artists on view, but because I realized I couldn't name ten female artists myself – let alone any working over 100 years ago.

That night, I couldn't sleep. I began an Instagram page and called it 'The Great Women Artists'. The aim then, as it still is now, was to share the work of women artists.

And now I've put it into a book. This is a celebration of women in art from the 1500s to the present day. But it can also be your guide to art history, helping you understand and appreciate the works.

Who knows, maybe it will encourage you to make some art, too!

If you notice that a certain community or group of people aren't being talked about, do whatever you can (no matter how big or small) to make a difference. This could include drawing a picture, writing a story or telling your teachers that they've forgotten someone or something.

Before we wind back the clock to the 1500s, I want to tell you about a favourite artist of mine, who gave me the courage to do what I do now. Her name was **ALICE NEEL**. She was born in 1900, and lived for 84 years. She spent her life in New York City, painting people she knew, and those who lived nearby.

When we think of the people who were painted throughout history, they tend to be grand or famous, like kings and queens. Alice didn't care about that. She painted people of every background, and treated each one equally – from her landlord's son, Benjamin, when he was about 12 years old, to her famous artist friends, such as Andy Warhol. Her work taught me that everyone's portrait is worthy of being painted, and their story is worthy of being included in art history. Because if you leave people out, you're not truly representing the world.

YOU'RE ALSO MISSING OUT ON GREAT ART!

It's OK not to like all the artworks in this book. Art's power isn't in whether it's liked or not. It's about showing another side to a story, starting a conversation and allowing people to express themselves. Also, do remember that we live long lives. If a picture doesn't speak to you now, maybe it will when you're older, or when you've gone through certain experiences.

THE ART HISTORIAN'S TOOLBOX

HOW TO LOOK AT ARTWORKS

There is no right or wrong answer when it comes to talking about art. Try to reflect on the experiences you've had in your life so far. Perhaps looking at an artwork might remind you of a film you saw, a conversation you had, or a field you passed by on the train.

Remember, you're also looking at the art at a certain date and time. That, too, is really interesting. How might you feel, looking at this work as someone in the 2020s? What might it tell you about your life now?

WHAT TO ASK

You can also think about how people might have viewed artworks over the centuries. Ask yourself: What was it like to see this picture at the time it was made? It's incredible that artworks sit there in stillness, day after day, yet through our minds and eyes we can give them new meaning by thinking about how they make us feel.

WHERE CAN WE FIND ARTWORKS?

Artworks can call many places home: in the museum, on your kitchen fridge, at the train station, parks, in your classroom. Anyone can make an artwork, and put together an art exhibition (where art is displayed, to be viewed by an audience). It's all about telling a story through pictures. Why don't you try it? You can make an exhibition with artworks made by you and your friends, hung on a wall at school, or at home.

WHY IS ART HISTORY SO IMPORTANT?

If you like science and maths, why should you like art history? Because art history encompasses everything! I like to see it as an umbrella that covers many different subjects. Think about it: What if there's a painting of your favourite author? That's literature and art! Or what if an artwork is made out of something technological, or deals with the environment? That's art and science!

The possibilities are endless. Never forget that. If your friends say they're not into art, try discussing what I've just told you with them.

THE BEST PART OF ART HISTORY IS GOING TO SEE THE WORKS FOR YOURSELF. Art museums are the greatest treasure chests, full of endless objects, artworks and stories, where we can learn not just about the people who came before us, but how they saw the world. A great first step is looking at art in a book, or on a museum website, and maybe one day you can see them in person yourself, which is best of all.

THE RENAISSANCE: PORTRAITURE AND STILL LIFE

AROUND 500 YEARS AGO, THE WORLD WAS A VERY DIFFERENT PLACE. There was no electricity, no screens, no lights, no cars. But it was especially different for half the world's population: women. They had very few rights compared to men. Ridiculously, at this time, women's brains were considered inferior, and their role mainly involved doing tasks around the home (cooking, cleaning, raising children).

Women couldn't travel on their own, or earn money, and they didn't have a say in anything when it came to politics. In Britain, it took until 1918 for women to be allowed to vote, and in France this didn't happen until 1944. So you can only imagine how much worse it was for women in the 1500s and 1600s.

THERE WERE ALSO RESTRICTIONS ON WOMEN'S EDUCATION, WHICH MEANT ART EDUCATION TOO.

Despite campaigning for centuries, women were not allowed to attend free art schools until the 1800s. And it took until the 1890s for them to be allowed to draw the nude figure from life – which means drawing a real person (not someone in a painting or photograph) without any clothes on.

Drawing a nude person from life is called **LIFE DRAWING**.

But why do they have no clothes on? Sounds funny, doesn't it? But studying the body like this meant that the artist could draw or paint the bodies in all sorts of imagined clothes, and into lots of different scenes, from theatrical poses to epic battles.

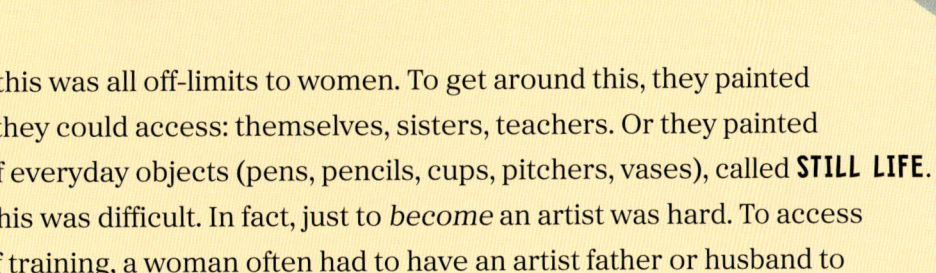

However, this was all off-limits to women. To get around this, they painted whatever they could access: themselves, sisters, teachers. Or they painted pictures of everyday objects (pens, pencils, cups, pitchers, vases), called **STILL LIFE**. But even this was difficult. In fact, just to *become* an artist was hard. To access any sort of training, a woman often had to have an artist father or husband to teach her the tricks of the trade. Or she had to come from a wealthy family able to hire private art teachers.

STILL LIFE
A still life is a picture of man-made or natural objects. Still-life art can include anything from a plate full of fish to a single apple, a coffee pot to a vase of flowers.

But, against all the odds, some women thrived. They might have been restricted to painting **PORTRAITS** or still lifes, but they tackled these art styles with ambition and creativity.

PORTRAIT
A portrait is a picture of a person or group of people. A self-portrait is a picture of the person who made it.

An artist called **SOFONISBA ANGUISSOLA** is a great example of someone who did brilliant things with different art styles. She was born in Italy in 1532, the eldest of six sisters and one brother.

Here is a painting (or you could say, a 'group portrait', if you were being fancy) of Sofonisba's siblings playing chess. Look at how she combines different styles into one painting. We have the landscape at the back (the misty, mountainous backdrop); still life (the chessboard); and portraiture (her sisters and the maid, the grey-haired lady peering in at the right-hand side).

SOFONISBA ANGUISSOLA, *THE GAME OF CHESS*, 1555.

> I love how adoringly the younger sister is gazing at the older one (it reminds me of how much I idolized my sisters!).

When it came to portraits, Sofonisba was also clever in the way she played around with the traditional roles of man and woman, teacher and student. Let's look at her work *Bernadino Campi Painting Sofonsiba Anguissola* – a painting of herself and her teacher.

SOFONISBA ANGUISSOLA, *BERNARDINO CAMPI PAINTING SOFONSIBA ANGUISSOLA,* c. 1559.

> Notice how she's painted herself nearly twice as big as him. Don't you think it makes her appear far more superior? He's also painting a detail on her jacket, which is a task that teachers normally gave to their pupils! It's as if the artist wanted to assign her teacher the same homework he gave her! Then, most daringly of all, look at how her left hand is guiding his around the canvas. Could this be the moment the student becomes the teacher?

Sofonisba lived during a period called the **RENAISSANCE**, which took place in Europe from the 1300s to about 1600.

The word *renaissance* means 'rebirth' or 'revival'. This was a time when architects, artists and poets were 'rediscovering' the ancient Greeks and Romans, who were around nearly 2,000 years before, in a time known as the 'Classical era'. Renaissance artists wanted to copy the classical style.

In art, this meant creating 'lifelike' people and scenes. To achieve a lifelike scene, **PERSPECTIVE** was key. This involved working out how to recreate the 3D world on a flat, 2D surface.

Let's try it together. Look up from where you are reading. How do you draw what you see in front of you on a flat piece of paper, but make it look 3D?

You will need to find the furthest point away from you (known as the vanishing point). In your picture, make this the smallest detail. The point in your picture that is closest to you will be the largest detail. This makes a drawing look 3D.

We can see Sofonisba working in this way in *The Game of Chess*, where the landscape looks as if it is behind the figures.

An artist also had to be good at light and dark shading. This helped to make a painting look even more realistic.

SCULPTORS OF THE RENAISSANCE WERE ALSO KEEN ON WORKING IN LIFELIKE WAYS.

PROPERZIA DE' ROSSI was born in Bologna, Italy, in 1490 (where she was known for getting into trouble with the police!). She spent her time hand-carving detailed scenes in wood, as seen in the picture below on the left.

PROPERZIA DE' ROSSI, *JOSEPH AND POTIPHAR'S WIFE*, 1525-26 (LEFT). *GRASSI FAMILY CREST*, 1510-30 (RIGHT).

She worked on miniscule scales, too. These hand-carved scenes of saints are made from peach and plum stones!

Properzia was luckier than most women of the time. Her hometown, Bologna, was the first city in Italy to allow women to go to university. Those in charge of the city also encouraged women artists to make **SELF-PORTRAITS** and sign the paintings they'd created with their name.

You might be thinking, *well, obviously*. But back then, it wasn't so common. And even when women did sign their name, it didn't stop those who sold the art from scratching out women's names and replacing them with men's names, to make the art more valuable. Sadly, in those times a man's work sold for a lot more money than a woman's.

CLARA PEETERS was never going to let anyone steal her work. Born in Antwerp, Belgium, in 1594, Clara painted still lifes featuring glistening goblets, flowers, shells and china bowls.

 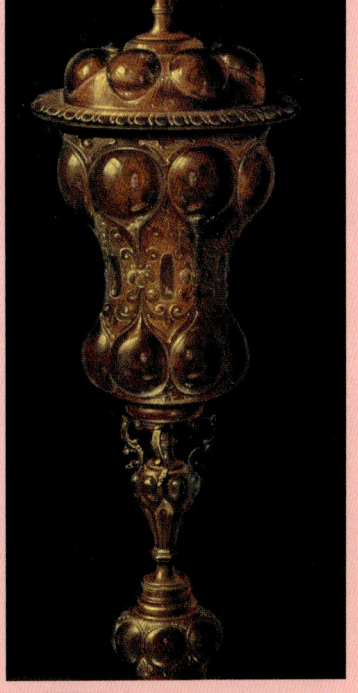

CLARA PEETERS, *STILL LIFE WITH A VASE OF FLOWERS, GOBLETS AND SHELLS*, 1612 (LEFT). DETAIL OF THE RIGHT-HAND GOBLET (RIGHT).

This painting might seem like a normal still life, but hidden in the grooves of the goblet on the right are reflections of a staggering ten self-portraits! It's as if, 400 years later, Clara is giving us a secret message: she is the painter.

ART TASK
Why don't you try to secretly paint a self-portrait into a picture of something else?

There was no stopping women from finding clever ways around the restrictions placed on them during this time. They proved that they were just as capable as their male counterparts, and should be celebrated as brilliant artists, too!

GIOVANNA GARZONI, *DOG WITH A BISCUIT AND A CHINESE CUP*, 1640s.

Women artists were also excellent at painting dogs. This gleaming-eyed canine is painted by Italian artist Giovanna Garzoni. Did you spot its rather grand bauble-studded collar?

BAROQUE AND BOTANY

'I'LL SHOW YOU WHAT A WOMAN CAN DO.'
– ARTEMISIA GENTILESCHI

As we leave the Renaissance and enter the 1600s, things in Europe get dramatic. Countries on the northern side of Europe (like England and the Netherlands) began breaking away from the Catholic Church. So, in response, the Catholic Church did everything it could to keep people following its faith.

The most effective way of doing this? Storytelling, of course. So artists painted biblical scenes, which, at times, could be bloody and terrifying (think scary movies, but 400 years ago). Even simple stories were told in dramatic pictures.

This was a style called the **BAROQUE**. And the paintings of this era included stormy skies, pitch-black backdrops, and bold, contrasting light effects.

Because of the success of the women we learned about in the previous chapter, women artists in the 1600s could become celebrities. And while women in the Renaissance tended to picture themselves as 'poised' and 'elegant', those in the seventeenth century had a different attitude. They appear strong and unafraid.

The greatest artist of this era was the mighty **ARTEMISIA GENTILESCHI**. She was born in Rome in 1593, the eldest daughter in an artistic family. When she was 12 her mother died, so she was tasked with raising her three younger brothers. As her father was an artist, they hung out together in his studio, which was where Artemisia fell in love with painting and learned how to mix paint from pigment.

DID YOU KNOW?
Back then, paint tubes didn't exist, so artists had to crush rocks to make a powder, known as pigment. They mixed this with egg or water to turn it into liquid paint.

Artemisia was known for her daring and dramatic paintings. Take a look at this work: *Judith and her Maidservant with the Head of Holofernes*. It's of the brave biblical character, Judith, who, along with her maidservant, Abra, has just murdered the evil army general Holofernes to save her city from invasion.

Here, Artemisia paints moments after this happened. Judith, in her grand yellow dress, still grips a sharp sword in her hand, which she used to cut off Holofernes's head. You can just about make it out at the bottom. It could be something out of a horror movie!

The painting measures nearly 1.9m high – the same height as a very tall man.

ARTEMISIA GENTILESCHI, *JUDITH AND HER MAIDSERVANT WITH THE HEAD OF HOLOFERNES*, 1623–25.

Artemisia was very good at creating dramatic atmospheres in her paintings. She did this by using light and dark shading. Notice how she's lit the scene with just a single candle, which Judith seems to be covering with her hand. It makes me think that the scene is full of silence, with the women tip-toeing around so as not to get caught in the pitch-black of night.

Artemisia became so famous that people even drew pictures of her hand! She was also a smart businesswoman and demanded that she was paid the same as male artists (too right!).

ARTEMISIA GENTILESCHI, *SELF-PORTRAIT AS SAINT CATHERINE OF ALEXANDRIA*, c. 1615–17.

This is Artemisia in her **SELF-PORTRAIT AS SAINT CATHERINE OF ALEXANDRIA**, *a fourth-century saint who survived torture, and stood defiantly against evil. Her calm gaze tells me that good will triumph.*

I like Artemisia's work because she focuses on the woman's side of the story, making them heroic in a world that only really celebrated men.

ART TASK
Artists liked to paint themselves as someone else in self-portraits. Have a go at doing it yourself. Who would you like to dress up as?

The Baroque style was very influential. Artists all over Europe were inspired to create dramatic scenes, using techniques that showed stunning light effects. These can make us feel like we're watching a whole scene play out before our eyes, even though the painting is still and silent.

The Dutch provinces (now the Netherlands) in Northern Europe were also home to a population who loved art. But unlike Rome, they preferred **SECULAR SUBJECTS**.

SECULAR SUBJECTS
Non-religious subjects – such as portraits of people and objects that aren't connected to a famous Bible story.

Art was very popular in the city of Haarlem in the Dutch provinces. It was also the birthplace of **JUDITH LEYSTER** (born 1609). She was the eighth child of a brewer and went on to become an artistic star. Her name actually means 'lodestar' in Dutch – a type of star that can be used for navigation, like the North Star. Judith signed her work with her initials, 'JL', and a star.

This is Judith, aged 21, at her easel, smiling and painting a merry violinist.

It's worth saying that I don't think Judith's everyday work clothes included a giant lace ruff and an extravagant dress! By painting herself wearing a ruff, a symbol of wealth and high status, she was showing us how successful she was as an artist.

JUDITH LEYSTER, *SELF-PORTRAIT*, c. 1630.

Look closely at Judith's hands. Notice how many paintbrushes she has, which shows how many were required to make one painting. It also shows how skilful she was at choosing the right paintbrush for different parts of her picture.

Like Artemisia, Judith painted scenes that look like they're illuminated by a single light. She called this one **THE SERENADE**.

The man's lips are just about open, as if he's getting ready to burst into a fireside song.

JUDITH LEYSTER, *THE SERENADE*, 1629.

It wasn't only pictures of people that could be full of drama. **RACHEL RUYSCH**, who was born in 1664 in The Hague (about an hour's drive from Haarlem), painted flowers so lifelike they look as though they are breathing – or perhaps bursting out of their buds!

Rachel's bouquets were popular because they were supposed to be 'impossible'. In other words, her paintings mixed flowers from different seasons, so they wouldn't have been in bloom at the same time. But Rachel was able to paint these different flowers because her father owned a museum that embalmed living things – flowers, plants and even body parts.

EMBALMING
A process that involves covering things in chemicals, so they can be kept looking perfect all year round.

RACHEL RUYSCH, *STILL LIFE WITH FLOWERS ON A MARBLE TABLETOP*, 1716.

Looking at this painting by Rachel is a bit like watching a play. Each flower is a character: the red and white ones are our leading actors, with a chorus of flowers behind them.

RACHEL MADE OVER 250 PAINTINGS, AND ALSO HAD TEN CHILDREN!

Born in the west of England in 1700, **MARY DELANY** started out as a seamstress, sewing flowers on to her friend's jackets. But when she was 70 years old, she saw a red geranium beside a red piece of paper, and was inspired. She became a pioneer of collage, and she went on to produce more than 1,000 flower collages!

COLLAGE
A technique involving the cutting and pasting of paper, which is put together to make a picture.

Collage can be a great way of capturing the life of flowers, making them seem realistic. Think about how many layers of petals there can be on a flower. Try doing the same with paper – adding coloured layers to build up a picture – and you can end up with something that looks just like a flower.

MARY DELANY, *GERANIUM ZONALE* (LEFT), *SEA DAFFODIL* (CENTRE), *PASSIFLORA QUADRANGULARIS* (RIGHT), 1778.

Mary's collages of flowers feel so characterful. The dark backgrounds remind me of those earlier Baroque works, but these pictures feel three-dimensional.

Another artist who broke new ground in the natural world was **MARIA SIBYLLA MERIAN**, born in Germany in 1647. In 1691, she set sail from Amsterdam to South America. She was an entomologist (someone who studies insects) and in South America she sketched and painted creatures that Europeans had never seen before. These included creepy-crawly spiders, blooming butterflies and a host of glorious insects.

As in art, women in science have often been overlooked throughout history. So it's amazing to think that a woman's detailed drawings helped Europeans learn about species from across the globe.

MARIA SIBYLLA MERIAN, *POMEGRANATE AND MENELAUS BLUE MORPHO BUTTERFLY*, 1702–3.

Whether they were recreating large-scale biblical scenes or painting pictures of flowers, during the Baroque (and beyond!) women always came up with ways of seeing things anew.

BREAKING THE GLASS CEILING

NEOCLASSICISM

In London, there's a gallery called the Royal Academy of Arts. It's attached to an art school where pupils can study for free, and is run by famous artists called 'Royal Academicians' (also known as 'RAs'). It opened in 1768, at the height of **NEOCLASSICISM**.

NEOCLASSICISM

Neoclassicism is an art movement that celebrated the ancient past. Neo means 'new' or 'revived'. And classical refers to art and architecture by the Ancient Greeks and Romans (as we learned about in the Renaissance). In Neoclassical art, you see lots of classical sculptures and architecture (such as columns or pillars), inspired by famous ancient Greek buildings.

ANGELICA KAUFFMAN was one of the thirty-six founders of the Royal Academy. She was also one of only two women founders (the other was **MARY MOSER**).

ANGELICA KAUFFMAN, *DESIGN*, 1778-80.

Look at this round painting by Angelica, painted in 1778-80. It is called **DESIGN** and shows a woman studying a nude plaster cast of a male body, set against classical columns. At this time, women were banned from drawing a real nude body, but this painting shows how they got around the issue – by studying sculptures.

CAST
A *cast* is the result of a technique called *casting*, which is when artists mould an object (or a body) to make a sculpture.

But when the Royal Academy founders were first painted in the group's first official portrait, by Johann Zoffany, Mary and Angelica could hardly be seen in the picture...

Let's look at the official portrait closely. Can you spot Mary and Angelica?

JOHANN JOSEPH ZOFFANY, *THE ACADEMICIANS OF THE ROYAL ACADEMY*, 1771–72.

While we can see all the men in their colourful suits and extravagant wigs, surrounding the nude models on the right, Angelica and Mary are nowhere to be found. Direct your eyes to the top right-hand corner though, and you'll see them pictured as painted portraits hung on the wall!

But Angelica was clearly too busy working hard to be fazed by this. As a young girl born in Switzerland in 1741, and growing up in Lombardy (now Italy, then under Austrian rule), she was a child prodigy. She could speak five languages, sing beautifully, and make art.

ANGELICA KAUFFMANN, *SELF-PORTRAIT AS SINGER, HOLDING A SHEET OF MUSIC*, 1753.

Here is a self-portrait of Angelica holding a sheet of music and showing off her various talents. It was painted when she was just 12 years old!

Angelica was able to become an artist because her father was a painter. He gave her private art lessons and took her to see the European Old Masters (large, grand paintings of classical and biblical stories). Aged 25, she moved to London and set up a studio, where she demanded prices for her art that matched those of her male contemporaries.

In her art, Angelica often painted famous classical stories from a female perspective. Instead of painting women as passive (which means they are not actively making their own decisions), she gave them power, showing them negotiating with men and speaking with them as equals.

But while Angelica was a trailblazer, it took until 2024, over 200 years after she died, for her to have a solo exhibition at the Royal Academy!

SPOTLIGHT: NEEDLEWORK

While it's much better today, the Royal Academy wasn't always a kind place to women. For example, eighteen months after opening, they banned artists who used needlework, as this was considered 'craft' or 'decoration', and not (in their opinion) 'real' art. This was very unfair, because for much of history women had been limited to just this type of art.

So, I thought I'd spotlight artists working in different styles of needlework, from quilt-making to embroidery, over the centuries. These are women I believe deserved a place at the Royal Academy, but who were never given the chance.

EMMA CIVEY STAHL, *WOMAN'S RIGHTS QUILT*, c. 1875.

In the 1800s, women were fighting for their rights like never before, in what is known as the **SUFFRAGE MOVEMENT** (which you can learn more about on page 41).

In the above quilt, **EMMA CIVEY STAHL** (born 1860, in Iowa or Illinois, USA) pictures women riding horses and carts or speaking to an audience – activities they were almost always banned from doing. She also shows men at home looking after the kids. While that is very normal for men to do today, during this time it was rare. Dotted with beautiful flowers and leaves, Stahl's quilt shows us what can blossom if we strive for an equal society.

HARRIET POWERS was born into slavery (which we will learn more about on page 77) in Georgia, USA, in 1837. After becoming a freewoman in the second half of the 1800s, she turned to quilt-making, alongside raising nine children.

Through her quilts, Harriet told a collection of stories, from those found in the Bible (can you spot *Jonah and the Whale*?) to local legends, such as the time her neighbourhood froze over because it was so cold. She called that particular panel *Cold Thursday* and, in the bottom-left square, you can see all the animals surrounded by snow.

HARRIET POWERS, *PICTORIAL QUILT*, 1895–98.

What other scenes and animals can you spot?

VICTORIAN BRITAIN: NEW PROGRESSIONS AND NEW INVENTIONS

Throughout Queen Victoria's reign, from 1837 to 1901, Britain experienced huge changes. New technologies, such as the camera and improvements in printing techniques whizzed art into the future. But some of the biggest changes were new freedoms for women.

DID YOU KNOW?

In 1842, *The Illustrated London News* became the world's first illustrated newspaper, which meant pictures, illustrations and paintings could be seen by more people than ever before.

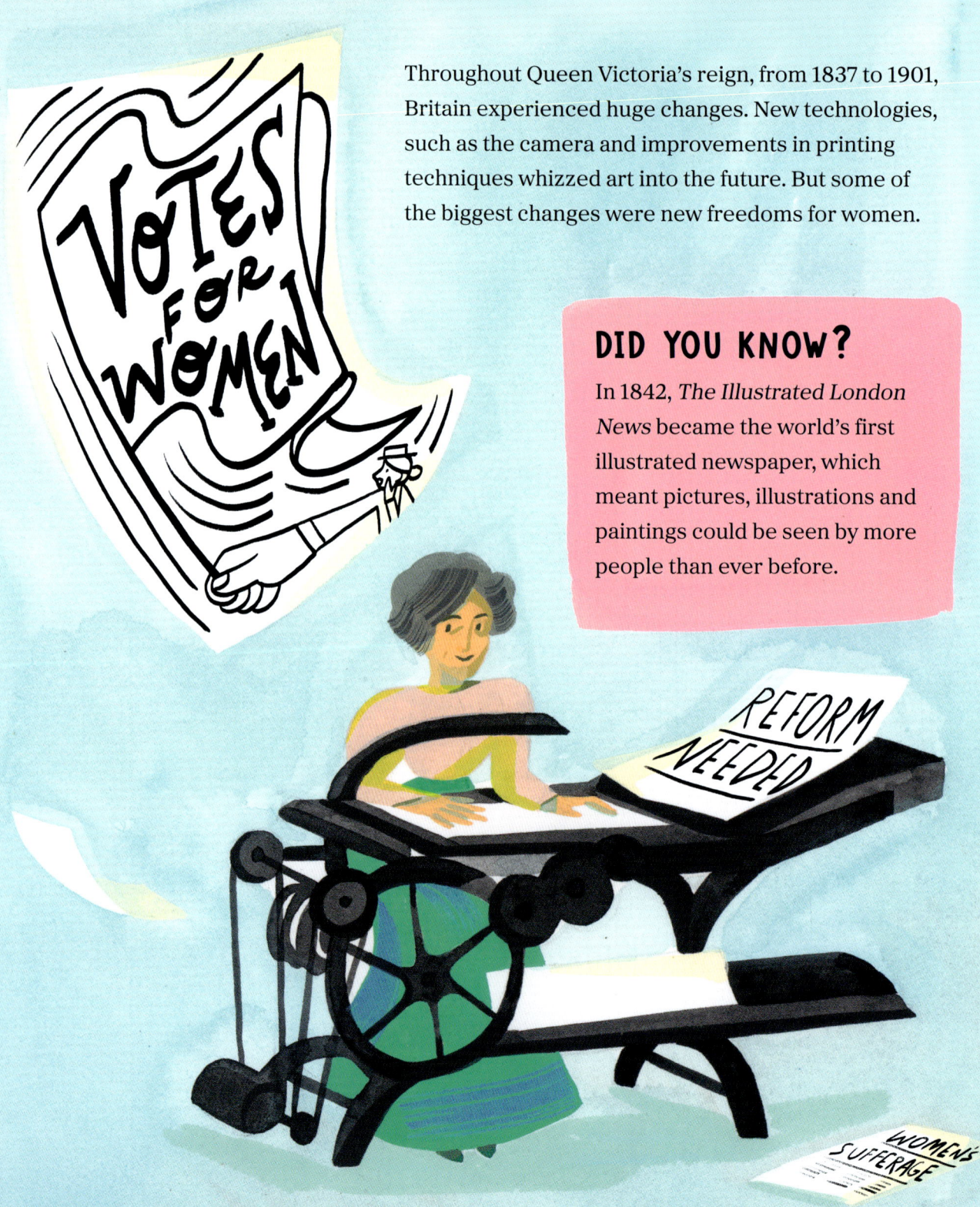

As we've learned, the past wasn't an easy place for a woman to be an artist. There was also, at this time, a law that stated women had no separate legal identity from their husbands, meaning that they had little control over their lives and money. Women couldn't vote, and they didn't even have access to proper education.

Taking matters into their own hands, women campaigned for equality. They fought for their right to vote in elections, so they could have a say in how the country was run. These women – and the men who agreed with them – were known as the **SUFFRAGISTS**.

Some women who supported the suffragists were artists. Art can be a powerful tool to express the struggles that people are experiencing in their lives.

EMILY MARY OSBORN, born in London in 1828, understood this. She was closely involved with the fight for women's rights, as well as being a successful artist who ran her own painting studio. In 1857, she painted *Nameless and Friendless*, which, to me, sums up what life must have been like for most Victorian women.

Look at this painting carefully. What do you see?

A woman is in a busy art dealer's shop. Through the window, we can see stormy skies and rain pouring down. Inside, men are active – on ladders, writing down records and inspecting pictures.

The two men in top hats in the corner appear confused at the sight of a woman in the shop.

EMILY MARY OSBORN, *NAMELESS AND FRIENDLESS*, 1857.

How do you think the woman looks? To me, she seems sad and lonely. She is pale, dressed in black, probably to signify her mourning (Victorian women wore black after their husbands or family members had died), and her expression is sorrowful. This is very different to the upright, confident and rosy-cheeked boy beside her.

Across the counter, a man is inspecting a picture. Maybe it's by the woman, or belongs to her. Either way, it seems like she's hoping to make some money, or to perhaps be taken seriously as an artist.

Emily created this picture to demonstrate how men were able to work and enjoy their lives, while women struggled. She is showing how unfair and broken the world can be.

Humour was another good method for highlighting injustice. *Woman's Work: A Medley*, painted in 1861 by **FLORENCE CLAXTON** (born in 1838 in Italy, but a British artist), makes fun of how ridiculous it was for women to be treated worse than men, just because of their gender.

FLORENCE CLAXTON, 'WOMEN'S WORK': A MEDLEY, 1861.

> In the centre is a lazy, rather smug man on a throne, surrounded by women. On the right, we see a woman knocking on a door. Perhaps this is meant to show her permanently locked out of the world of work. On the left, women are pointing towards the open horizon, as if searching for job opportunities (because there were none available to women!).

Emily and Florence were both ardent supporters of a woman's right to proper art education. And their campaigning worked. In 1861, the Royal Academy Schools agreed to admit women students. In 1871, London's Slade School of Fine Art opened for men and women on equal terms. Women could even paint nude bodies! This changed women's access to art forever, and it was thanks to these tireless campaigners of the nineteenth century that opportunities for female artists soared in the twentieth century.

NEW INVENTIONS: THE CAMERA

While today you might be able to photograph and film on a phone, the world back in Victorian times was a very different place.

In the early 1800s, artists were still trying to paint and draw people and places as realistically as possible. But gradually that changed.

Why? Partly because a new tool had been invented: the camera, which meant there was less of a need for realistic paintings.

In ancient times, people used something called a camera obscura, which means a 'darkened room'. On one side of the room, there was a small hole in the wall. Sunlight bounced off objects outside the camera obscura and passed through this hole. Then the image on the outside was reflected on the wall, upside down. But these images were just temporary – they couldn't be kept forever.

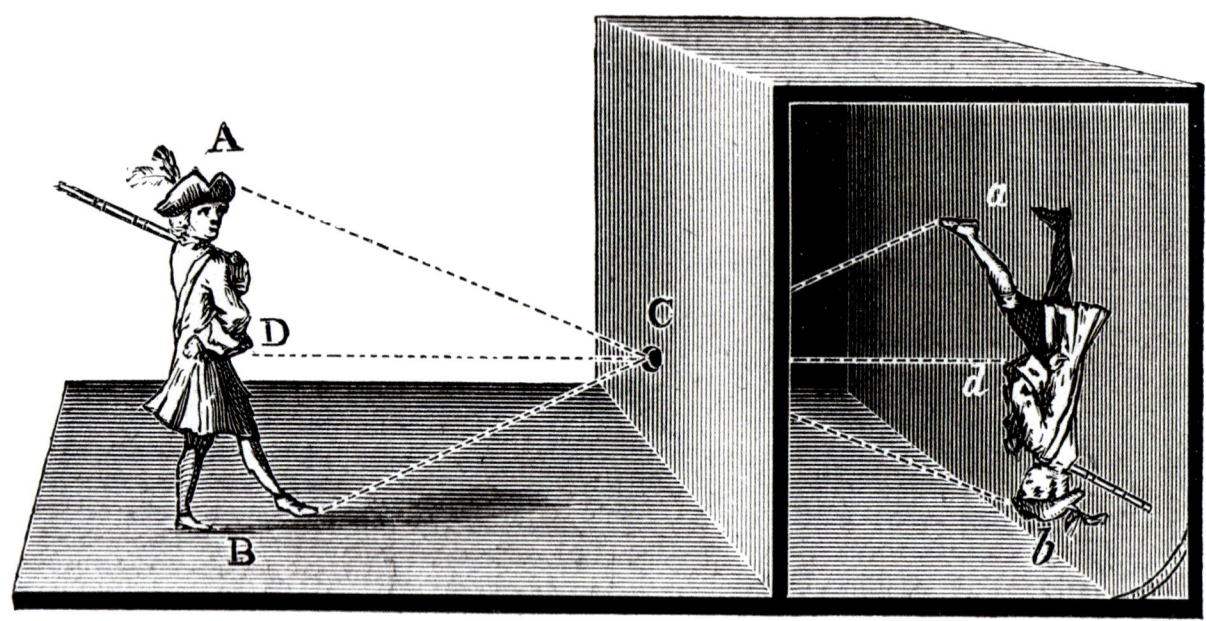

AN EXAMPLE OF HOW A CAMERA OBSCURA WORKS.

In 1816, French inventor Joseph Nicéphore Niépce created the first 'photograph'. He used the camera obscura technique but projected the image on to a piece of paper coated in silver chloride. And – success! The reflection was transferred on to the paper.

Not long after, the camera started to be used as a tool for art. Unlike today, these cameras were big machines, and often required their subject to be very still.

> While painting and sculpture had always been dominated by men, the camera was new. Women, although still at a disadvantage, could therefore make photography their own, without being compared unfairly to the men who'd come before them.

JULIA MARGARET CAMERON was born to English and French parents in India in 1815. In 1845, she settled in England with her family, at a time when exciting possibilities for the camera were being explored by artists.

Julia was 48 when she first picked up a camera (it was a present from her daughter), and she soon became a pioneer of taking pictures of people – known as **PORTRAIT PHOTOGRAPHY**.

This was Julia's camera. Do you see any similarities to the cameras we have today?

Julia mastered a style that made her subjects look bohemian and angelic. Think long hair, headbands, white robes and flowers! She also used a lot of light, which gave her pictures a hazy glow.

One of her favourite people to snap was Alice Liddell, the inspiration for Lewis Carroll's 1865 book *Alice's Adventures in Wonderland*.

JULIA MARGARET CAMERON, *THE ROSEBUD GARDEN OF GIRLS*, 1868.

JULIA MARGARET CAMERON, *POMONA*, 1872.

Here is Alice dressed as Pomona, the Roman goddess of gardens and fruit trees.

Julia was part of a much bigger artistic circle called the **PRE-RAPHAELITES,** who painted in a similar style to how she photographed.

Here's an example of a Pre-Raphaelite painting by Cameron's contemporary, **JOANNA MARY BOYCE** (a British artist, born in 1831). It's of Fanny Eaton, who was born a freewoman in Jamaica in 1835, one year after slavery was finally abolished in the British colonies.

JOANNA MARY BOYCE, *STUDY OF FANNY EATON,* 1861.

Fanny was one of the most famous artists' models of the time. She was known for her striking looks and beautiful high cheekbones. Dressed in a Greek-style gown, with a turquoise hairband, and sitting in a thoughtful pose, she appears like a painted version of Cameron's photographs.

EVELYN DE MORGAN, *NIGHT AND SLEEP,* 1878.

Or take a look this Pre-Raphaelite painting from 1878 by Evelyn De Morgan (an English painter born in 1855). It's of two figures flying through the sky, as if in a dream, emerging out of (or perhaps disappearing under) a cloak. Like Cameron's photographs, they appear almost divine.

CYANOTYPES (AND THE FIRST-EVER PHOTO-BOOK)

A few decades earlier, before the camera had been fully developed, artists were experimenting with something called 'photographic techniques'.

In 1843, **ANNA ATKINS**, the English artist and botanist (born in 1799), published the first book to ever contain photographic images. She called it *Photographs of British Algae: Cyanotype Impressions*. 'Algae' refers to living organisms like plants or seaweed. 'Cyanotype' was the photographic technique she used (*cyan* comes from the Greek word for 'blue', as the images came out blue!).

ANNA ATKINS, *CYANOTYPES OF BRITISH ALGAE*, 1843.

Don't these magical images remind you of plants growing deep underwater?

Anna used photosensitive paper to achieve this. She added more chemicals to this paper, placed it in a darkened room and then put the algae on top of the paper. When this was all exposed to light, the images were transferred on to the paper. Cyanotypes were born, and so was one of the first steps in making photographs.

PHOTOSENSITIVE PAPER is covered in chemicals that respond when they are exposed to light, creating a photograph that can be printed.

The progress women made from the start of Queen Victoria's reign to its end, in 1901, was transformational. Although it took until 1918 for them to get the vote in Britain, we must give thanks to these pioneering artists who championed the development of photography and paved the way for the next generation of women.

IMPRESSIONISM

Some pictures look like they've been painted in an instant, or smashed into shards of colour. Sometimes, the painting might look like it's moving – maybe because of the wisps of paint swirling around the canvas or the flickers of white that appear like sparkling reflections.

Paintings like this belong to a movement called Impressionism. The artists of this movement, working mainly in Paris in the late 1800s, liked to create an 'impression' of their subject, as opposed to something that looked realistic.

Back then, these artists were thought of as rebellious and were often dismissed by snooty art critics (who saw their work as too modern). They were even banned from some museums! So, these enterprising artists set up their own exhibitions in alternative places, like photography studios. The first of these exhibitions took place in 1874.

At this point in time, everything was changing. A new century was approaching and the **INDUSTRIAL REVOLUTION** was booming. This was a period of great change, when machines and new inventions came along such as cars, telephones and high-speed trains.

The camera was becoming popular, as was the new 'moving picture' (also known as films). Artists were inspired to capture the speed of a new world, and this helped pave the way for Impressionism.

Paris was at the centre of this movement. The city had been rebuilt and redesigned between 1853 and 1870 by a man named Georges-Eugène Haussmann. Narrow medieval streets had been replaced with sweeping boulevards (long, wide roads). Embellished, ornate details had also been added to street lamps and Métro stations. Grand theatres were built to serve French high society – known as the *bourgeoisie*.

BERTHE AND EDMA MORISOT grew up in Paris in the 1840s and 1850s and were keen artists from a young age. Born into a well-off family, they had access to the best art tutors. In those days, however, young girls from this background were supposed to grow up to be well-to-do ladies. One tutor, stunned by their talents, even foresaw their artistic careers as a 'catastrophe'!

Sadly, Edma did indeed have to give up her artistic dreams when she got married. But Berthe carried on studying and became one of the most successful artists of the era. She was the only woman in the first Impressionist exhibition in 1874.

But while male artists could capture and explore the delights of the city, women were still restricted from going out alone. We can see this in Berthe's painting of Edma from 1869. Edma is shown sitting indoors, thinking, while looking down at her fan. Meanwhile, out of the window, onlookers can be seen on the balconies of a fancy building with green awnings. They get to enjoy the freedoms of the modern world, while Edma is stuck inside.

BERTHE MORISOT, *THE ARTIST'S SISTER AT A WINDOW*, 1884.

Don't you think the fan looks like it's made up of blotches of colour? It reminds me of paint on a palette. Perhaps Edma is pondering the life she might have lived if she hadn't given up art.

As the years edged closer to 1900, Berthe's thick brushwork became looser, and she painted with fast, slapdash marks. You can see this in her painting In the *Garden at Maurecourt*, 1884.

Doesn't this scene look hazy, like each strand of grass is dancing at an uncontrollable pace?

BERTHE MORISOT, *IN THE GARDEN AT MAURECOURT*, 1884.

Notice how Berthe is painting an outdoors scene, here. Portable paint tubes were also invented at this time, so artists no longer had to work inside their studios, and could set up their easels and paint outside (the French called it 'en plein air'). This picture was painted in a private garden – one of the rare places women could paint outside.

American artist **MARY CASSATT**, born in Pennsylvania, USA in 1844, was also part of the Impressionists. She also focused on the lives of women and girls. Her paintings included a girl relaxing in a blue chair beside her beloved dog, a mother (or carer) and child enjoying a goodnight hug, and a young teen engrossed in a book.

MARY CASSATT, *LITTLE GIRL IN A BLUE ARMCHAIR*, 1878 (LEFT). *MOTHER AND CHILD (A GOODNIGHT HUG)*, 1880 (RIGHT).

MARY CASSATT, *YOUNG GIRL READING*, 1894.

Can you see how Mary is playing with all sorts of textures? The girl's clear, filled-in face differs from the scratchy marks that make up the jumper and the book's pages.

What books do you think she is reading?

Through her work, Mary encouraged learning and education for women, but there were still many restrictions on what girls and women could do at this time. We can understand this if we read the diary of Impressionist artist **MARIE BASHKIRTSEFF** (born in what is now Ukraine, in 1858). During the 1880s, she wrote about her longing for freedom.

MARIE BASHKIRTSEFF, *SELF PORTRAIT WITH A PALETTE*, 1883.

'What I long for is the freedom of going about alone ... of stopping and looking at the artistic shops, of entering the museums ... that's the freedom without which one can't become a real artist ...'

You can tell Marie was ambitious. Just look at the determined gaze she painted in her self-portrait. Staring directly out at us, she has her paintbrush and palette at the ready, as if she is about to conquer the canvas – or the world.

The paintings by women Impressionists give us a glimpse into their lives. It shows how they used art to speak about and express themselves, how they demonstrated the love they had for their families, and their hopes for the future.

ART TASK
If you hope for something, have a go at drawing it. Sometimes we need to see it to believe it, and you never know how one picture may inspire the next generation.

EXPRESS YOURSELF

Have you ever looked at a painting (maybe even in this book) and thought: *Hang on, something doesn't look right. That colour doesn't match up to real life. Why is their skin green, and the sun blue? Why do their faces look so strange?*

The start of a new century, 1900, marked a new time for art. Artists were expressing themselves in ways they had never done before. Guided by their emotions, they used bright colours that reflected the way they felt about the world, rather than how it actually looked.

As the century progressed, new opportunities arose for women. They could travel freely, earn their own money and, in many places, vote. In their art, they expressed themselves in brand-new ways, too – from showing the world who they loved, to demonstrating how they wanted to live.

EXPRESSING THROUGH SHAPES AND COLOUR

SUZANNE VALADON hadn't always dreamed of becoming an artist. She was born in 1865 in Montmartre, Paris, to a single mother. To help the family earn money, she worked as an acrobat. But after she fell from a trapeze at the age of 15, she had to change career.

So she became an artists' model, posing for their paintings and drawings. After a while, Valadon was bored of being the person in the painting (often called the **SUBJECT**). She wanted to be the artist. While lots of her friends went to art school, she followed a different route. She learned by carefully observing those who drew and painted her. And guess what? She eventually became a very successful artist, working in a style that was full of expression.

I love her 1923 painting *The Blue Room*. It shows Suzanne expressing the freedoms suddenly available to modern women in the early 1900s, such as having her own home, wearing casual clothes, and doing whatever she liked. Hanging out in her bed in the afternoon, for instance!

SUZANNE VALADON, *THE BLUE ROOM*, 1923.

> Look how many colours she uses on the face. I can see pink, white, yellow, orange, red ... Suzanne liked to express how she felt through colour.

In 1911, at the age of 46, Suzanne had her first exhibition at a gallery run by Clovis Sagot (a former clown!). Her favourite subjects were flowers, self-portraits and cats.

SUZANNE VALADON, *RAMINOU AND PITCHER WITH CARNATIONS*, 1932.

I love how her cat is full of personality! If you have a pet or a favourite animal, how might you show their character in art?

EXPRESSING IDENTITY

Artists also used their art to express different identities. **CLAUDE CAHUN**, born 1894 in Nantes, France, used the camera – along with other tools and techniques (like the mirror) – for this very reason.

CLAUDE CAHUN, *SELF-PORTRAIT REFLECTED IN A MIRROR*, 1928.

Notice Claude's shaved head and masculine dress. Why do you think we see Claude's face twice – as a person and as a reflection in the mirror? It makes me think that Claude was exploring different identities.

CLAUDE CAHUN AND MARCEL MOORE, *UNTITLED (CLAUDE CAHUN IN LE MYSTÈRE D'ADAM [THE MYSTERY OF ADAM])*, 1929.

Claude also dressed as different characters for photographs, such as angels or aeroplane pilots. Perhaps Claude is showing us that these 'roles' don't have to be restricted to either men or women.

ART TASK

Art is a great tool to express our identity. What could you dress as, or pose in front of, to show the world how you see yourself or how you feel inside?

AMRITA SHER-GIL used art to express the deep love she had for her country. Although she was born in Budapest, Hungary in 1913, for much of her life she lived in India, where her father was from. Reflecting the blazing tones of India, a country famed for its bright colours and warm climate, she painted figures in fluorescent fabrics and glittering textures. Some of her subjects were family members, such as these girls, two of whom were her cousins.

AMRITA SHER-GIL, *THREE GIRLS*, 1935.

Look at this painting closely. To me, the three girls look like they're between childhood and adulthood. How do you think they are feeling? While they look very beautiful and grown-up, I sense that they are reflecting on their past, while also anticipating their future.

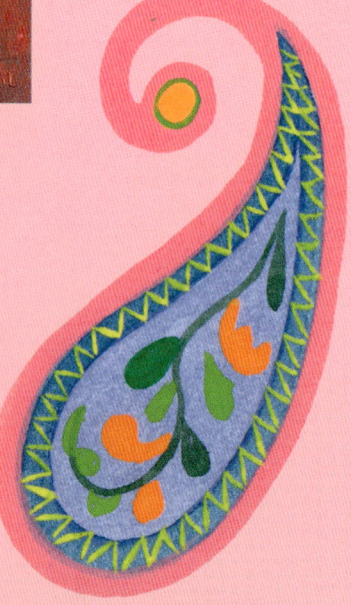

EXPRESSING LOVE

Artists also pictured themselves with their romantic partners, to express feelings of love.

GLUCK was born in 1895 in London and grew up in a strict, traditional Jewish family. Gluck liked to dress **ANDROGYNOUSLY** – which means wearing clothes typically meant for both men and women.

A hundred years ago, the world wasn't very accepting of people in queer relationships. Gluck, who was queer, paved the way for that change, by painting the first-known image of female gay love in British art history. In this painting, Gluck is in the foreground, with their lover, Nesta Obermer, shown behind.

You can tell that Gluck loved Nesta. Look at how Gluck has painted their heads conjoined as one. Unlike Gluck, who seems to be in shadow, Nesta is basking in a white glow, with her blonde hair framing Gluck's like a halo.

GLUCK, *MEDALLION (YOUWE)*, 1936.

Painting is a great way of showing love between people – whether it's a romantic relationship, a friendship or love between family members. While relationships might not last forever, a piece of art can be a reminder of the bond that people once had.

EXPRESSION IN ALL FORMS

Artists were also experimenting with *where* they painted. **VANESSA BELL**, born in London in 1879 (and the great-niece of Julia Margaret Cameron, see page 45), was known for her expressive paintings of friends and family, interiors and landscapes.

It became a meeting point for the a group of creative thinkers known as the **BLOOMSBURY GROUP**. (They were called this as they originally met in Vanessa's former house in Bloomsbury, in London, before moving to Charleston.)

The Bloomsbury Group were famous for making every aspect of their life about their art. This also applied to their home. Vanessa and her friend (and former lover) Duncan Grant painted every corner of the house!

Every fireplace, doorknob, bath, bookshelf and lampshade got the artistic treatment, and for her house she used the same colours (warm pinks, tomato red, bright blue, lime green) that she used for her paintings.

VANESSA BELL'S FORMER STUDIO AT CHARLESTON.

VANESSA BELL, BOOK COVER FOR 'THREE GUINEAS' BY VIRGINIA WOOLF, 1938.

Vanessa's sister was the famous writer Virginia Woolf. She often made the cover art for her sister's books!

The Bloomsbury Group were all about modern living. While they had grown up in a very traditional Victorian society, they wanted to leave these values behind and embrace the new world. At the dawn of a new century, they painted and created in ways people in England hadn't seen before now, and they never restricted themselves to just one art form.

MACHINES AND THE FIRST WORLD WAR

The dawn of the 1900s was also the dawn of many incredible inventions. Because of new technologies and the rise of industrialization, life began to speed up like never before. Millions of people moved from the countryside to the cities, where there were more job opportunities and many more houses were being built.

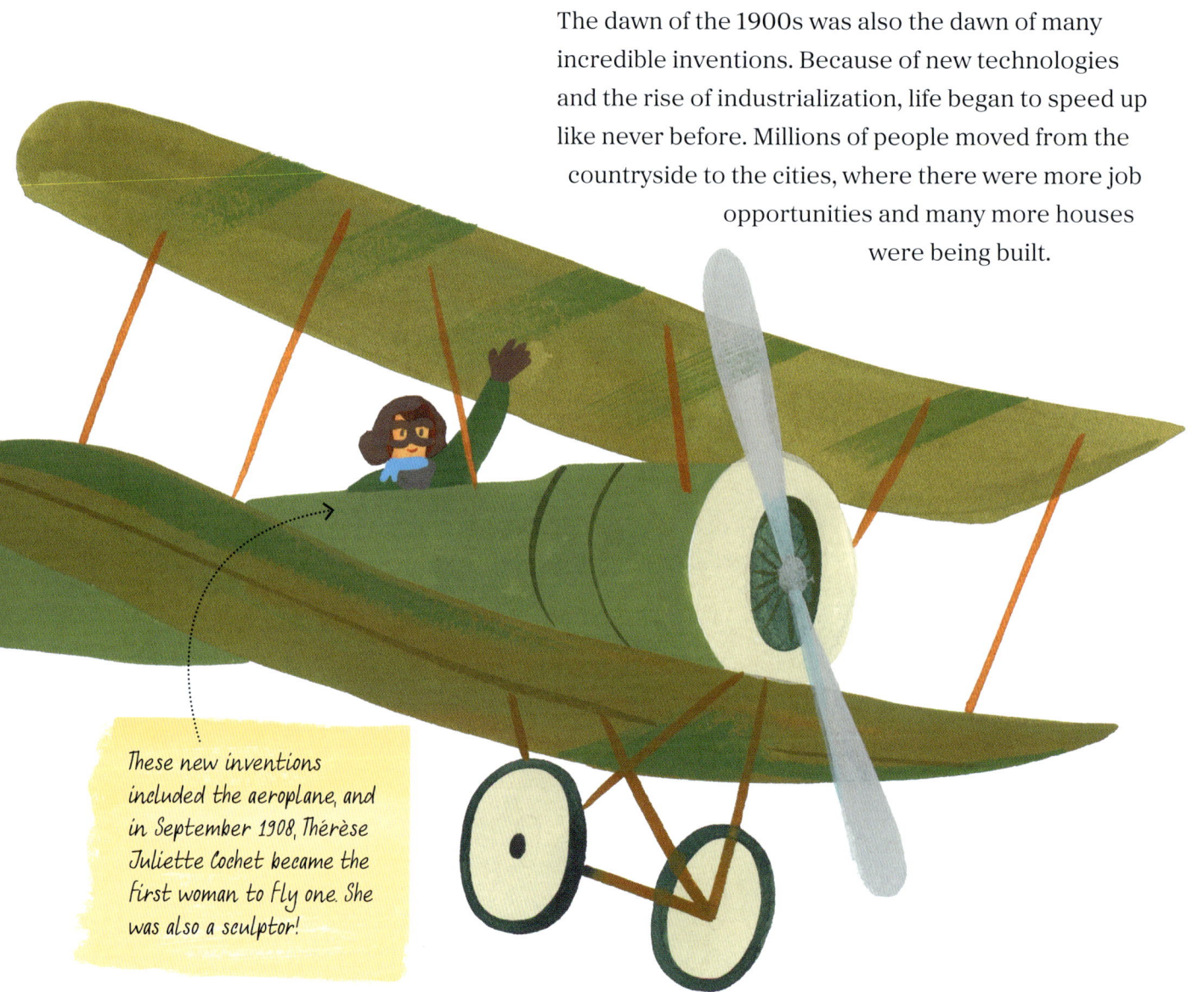

These new inventions included the aeroplane, and in September 1908, Thérèse Juliette Cochet became the first woman to fly one. She was also a sculptor!

Can you imagine being in a high-speed car for the first time? Or whizzing through the ocean on a motorboat? How about making a telephone call, instead of waiting weeks to receive a letter?

Artists were fascinated by these modern machines, and captured their effects – and the way they were changing people's lives – in art. Some did this with a technique called **ABSTRACTION**.

ABSTRACTION
Abstraction involves breaking up an image into shapes, lines and colours.

Have a look at this painting, **ELECTRIC PRISMS** by Sonia Delaunay. Sonia was born in Ukraine in 1885 but, like many artists, studied in Paris. Does it remind you of anything? What does the title suggest?

PRISM

A prism is a see-through 3D shape, with flat sides that can cause light to bend.

SONIA DELAUNAY, *ELECTRIC PRISMS*, 1914.

Notice how, in this painting, there is no specific image, and no beginning or end. See how it's made up of colourful shapes and lines? These are all features of abstraction.

Don't you think the strokes of colour also look a bit like musical notes? Artists at this time were fascinated by something called synaesthesia, which is when a person can hear sounds as if they were different colours!

WHAT DO YOU HEAR WHEN YOU LOOK AT THIS PAINTING?

Abstraction also allows the viewer to interpret what they see in their own way. When I look at this work, I feel like I'm in a car winding through a city, stopping at traffic lights, with street lamps all around me. What do you see?

63

The 1910s were also a dark time, clouded by the **FIRST WORLD WAR** (1914–18), which caused divisions between European countries. You can imagine the skies filled with grey planes shooting overhead and fierce battles breaking out across muddy fields. New machinery was needed in the war (like planes, for dropping bombs), and so new technology was appearing all the time, at lightning speed.

As the war approached, the colours in paintings faded from warm to cold, and the soft edges became hard and angular. Take this painting, *Cyclist*, by the Russian artist **NATALIA GONCHAROVA**, born in 1881.

NATALIA GONCHAROVA, *CYCLIST*, 1913.

Look at how she captures the speed of the cyclist's ferocious peddling through the flickers of white, black and grey coming off his bicycle wheels. You can almost hear them screech!

It looks like the cyclist is in a hurry. Do you ever rush around? I know the feeling!

Imagine trying to transform the watery ocean into slick, hard shapes. **BENEDETTA CAPPA MARINETTI**, born in Rome, Italy in 1897, did this with her painting *Speeding Motorboat*.

Benedetta was part of an art movement called **FUTURISM**. These artists looked to the future, glorified the modern world and set out to paint 'the beauty of speed'. They also took inspiration from the new, extraordinary views that aeroplanes offered.

BENEDETTA CAPPA MARINETTI, *SPEEDING MOTORBOAT*, 1923-24.

The viewpoint of this painting makes it seem like we're looking down at the boat from the sky. Maybe the yellow is the reflection of the plane in the water. By painting the boat in the distance, Benedetta is also showing us how quickly it can move.

DID YOU KNOW?

In 1932, several years after this painting was made, Amelia Earhart became the first woman to fly solo across the Atlantic Ocean.

While the First World War led to the invention of modern machines, it wasn't all positive. Also invented were tools of violence, which could kill people on a scale no one had seen before. Around 20 million people died. We can learn a lot about how the war affected innocent people from the art made at the time.

Artist **HANNAH HÖCH** was born in 1889 in Gotha, Germany, a country that was especially devastated after its defeat in the First World War. To represent its chaotic state, Hannah used collage to depict the country as a broken machine. With collage, artists can mix images of buildings, machines and real people, cut from different magazines and journals.

Hannah was a great supporter of women's rights. At the bottom right of this collage, you can see a map of Europe, where she has coloured in the countries that, at the time, still hadn't given women the right to vote.

HANNAH HÖCH, *CUT WITH THE DADA KITCHEN KNIFE THROUGH THE LAST WEIMAR BEER-BELLY CULTURAL EPOCH IN GERMANY*, 1919.

The level of harm caused by the war was indescribable and artists reacted to it with a type of art they called **DADA** – a word that didn't mean anything at all. The war seemed so senseless that only a nonsensical word could sum it up. Can you spot the word Dada in Hannah's work?

When you think about what war looks like, it's easy to just focus on the machines and battles. But ordinary people are affected by it, too. A German artist called **KÄTHE KOLLWITZ**, born in 1867 in the city Königsberg, which is now in Russia, was determined to show this suffering through her **PRINTMAKING**.

Käthe wanted to show the grief and fear people feel during war, and this print depicts women protecting their terrified children. I often think that world leaders who want to start a war should look at Käthe's work before making their decisions.

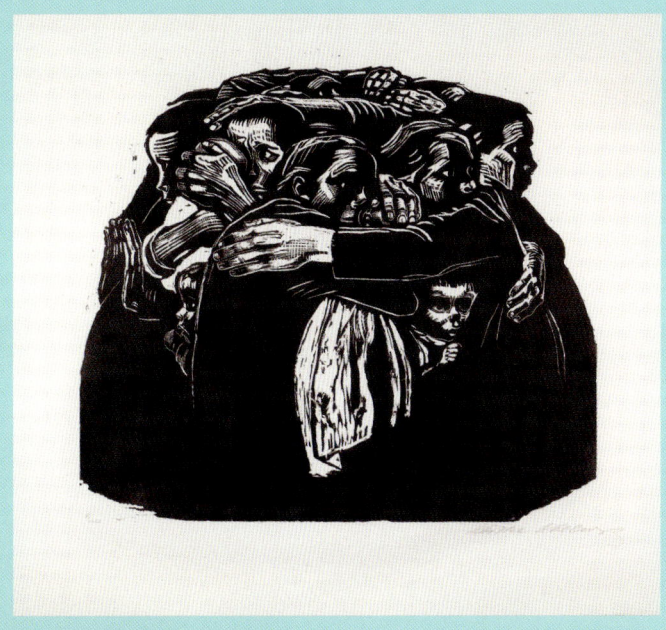

KÄTHE KOLLWITZ, *THE MOTHERS*, 1922.

Yet despite all the terror of the war, art and music flourished after it. In 1920s Germany, artists and musicians poured their emotions into their work. For a brief time (before the Second World War), it was a period of freedom and fun, and greater independence for women, as pictured by German artist **JEANNE MAMMEN** (born 1890).

JEANNE MAMMEN, *SHE REPRESENTS*, c. 1928.

Look at how this woman is even wearing a top hat and trousers, not a traditional ladies' dress — something only a modern woman would wear!

SURREALISM

'I'VE ALWAYS HAD ACCESS TO OTHER WORLDS. WE ALL DO BECAUSE WE DREAM.'
– LEONORA CARRINGTON

Have you ever thought about drawing your dreams? Capturing the wondrous, bizarre pictures that swirl around the inside of your head?

Let me introduce you to the **SURREALISTS**: a group of artists who took the images they found in the depths of their minds and transformed them into artworks. They drew mystical landscapes, sometimes with part-human or part-animal creatures. They created worlds that were just like ours, but were, at the same time, totally unfamiliar.

WHAT DOES THE WORD SURREAL ACTUALLY MEAN?
'Sur' means 'over' or 'above'. So adding it to 'real' is like saying something is slightly more than real, perhaps edging into fantasy.

Surrealism began in 1920s Paris, in the aftermath of the First World War. At this time, artists couldn't bear to think of the real world. After all, it was a place where – during the war – buildings had been destroyed, communities had been shattered, and soldiers were returning wounded from battle.

It was a broken world. A confusing and unfamiliar one, too. To make sense of what life had become, artists looked to their dreams.

Women artists were especially drawn to Surrealism. With it, they could invent new worlds, away from tradition and hierarchies where men were thought more important. Many artists had a rebellious and independent spirit, as they'd often fled strict, conservative families who insisted they give up their artistic lives to get married. But in Paris, they revelled in their new-found freedoms. They lived how they liked, and dressed the way they wanted. Dress (and dressing up – 'transforming' into something else) was very important to Surrealism. Some women artists wore bejewelled masks and lion-like headdresses to show off their eccentric personalities!

TRANSFORMATION

Transformation is very important to Surrealism. In Surrealist art, it might involve playing with what it meant to be a man or a woman. Or taking a symbol that had been seen as negative and giving it power. For example a witch might be presented as a positive role model, or a kitchen could be seen as a place of magic.

This is **LEONOR FINI**, who was born in Argentina in 1907, and lived in Italy and then Paris. Here she is, dressed like a figure we'd find in her paintings. She really is an embodiment of Surrealism.

LEONOR FINI AT A MASKED COSTUME BALL, 1951.

When Leonor was a young girl, she suffered from a case of conjunctivitis, which meant she had to have both eyes bandaged for months. According to legend, this allowed her to look deep into her imagination...

Here's an example of Fini's painting, which translates as **THE PASSENGER**. It's of a woman cloaked in a fantastical, glowing gown, who looks to be riding on a monstrous reptile. Where do you think she is travelling to?

LEONOR FINI, *LA PASSAGÈRE*, 1964.

Surrealist artists often make us look at traditional art – such as landscapes and portraits – in new ways. One of my favourite examples of someone who did this is Cornwall-based artist, **ITHELL COLQUHOUN**, who was born in India in 1906.

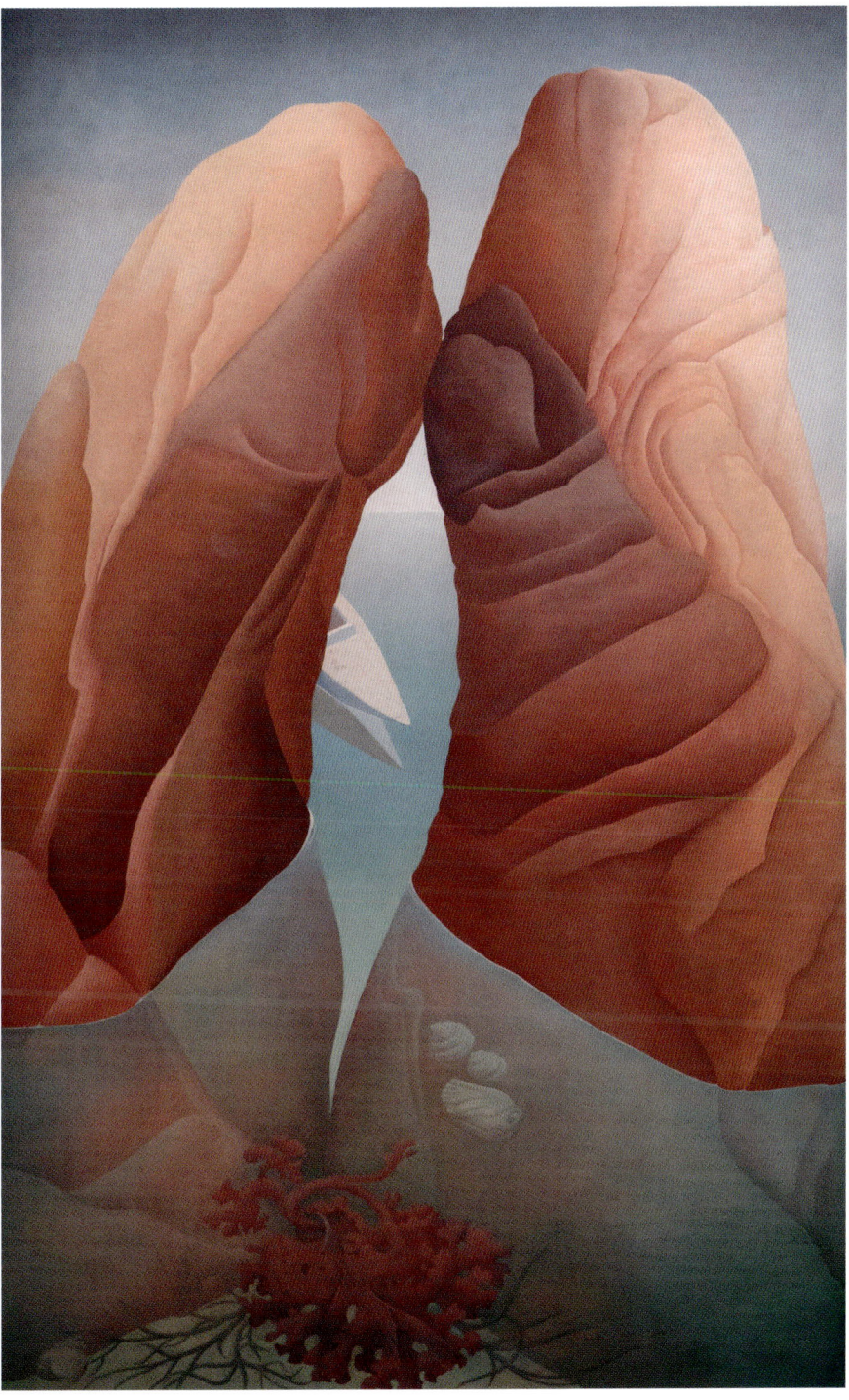

ITHELL COLQUHOUN, *SCYLLA*, 1938.

Have a look at Ithell's painting **SCYLLA** *from 1938. It looks like two rocks in a landscape, under-layered by a sprawling coral reef.*

Try looking again: ever glanced down at your legs in the bath, or by the sea? What do you see now?

Surrealists also played around with the traditional 'portrait'. You can see this in the paintings of **LEONORA CARRINGTON**, who was born in 1917 and raised in a big manor called Crookhey Hall in England. She ran away to Paris when she was just 20 years old, and eventually settled in Mexico City.

Here is her *Portrait of Max Ernst*, painted in 1939. Max and Leonora were lovers. Here, she pictures him with a bird-like coat, fishy tail and stripy clown-like socks. Walking through an icy landscape, he holds a green glass lantern with a trapped white horse inside. Look – it mirrors the frozen horse behind him.

The horse is inspired by Celtic legends that Carrington's Irish mother told her, of a creature that could fly through the air faster than the wind . . . Leonora saw the horse as her alter ego – a sort of second personality. But if the horse is trapped, what does this image tell us about how she might be feeling? Perhaps that as a woman with little opportunities, she feels stifled.

LEONORA CARRINGTON, *PORTRAIT OF MAX ERNST*, 1939.

> But could this also be Leonora taking control? At the time, women were typically thought of as muses, which meant they were the models in the painting, and the inspiration for male artists, rather than being artists themselves. By painting Max as her muse, Leonora is inventing a new world, transforming this idea. And maybe the horse in the green lantern isn't trapped, it's guiding Max forward.

Many Surrealists were obsessed with cats. At one time, Leonor Fini was looking after 17 of them.

The American artist **GERTRUDE ABERCROMBIE** (born in 1909) was inspired by cats, and also by the rhythm and improvisation of jazz. She lived in Chicago, where there was a big jazz scene.

GERTRUDE ABERCROMBIE, *THREE CATS*, 1956.

Gertrude often placed cats in eery scenes, representing them as a sequence, like in this 1956 painting, **THREE CATS**. Does it also make you think of the off-beat rhythms of jazz?

LEE MILLER, *SURGICAL GLOVES ARE STERILISED AND DRIED ON STANDS, CHURCHILL HOSPITAL, OXFORD, ENGLAND*, 1943.

Photography also played a key role in Surrealism, because it allowed artists to capture strange objects, or parts of them, in real-life scenarios. **LEE MILLER** was born in the USA in 1907, but lived her adult life in Paris, New York, Cairo and London – where she reported on the Second World War for a fashion magazine called *Vogue*, before moving to the English countryside.

Although she began taking surrealist photographs in 1929, Lee continued in this style when it came to taking her pictures of war – from women as pilots, to nurses sterilizing gloves in the hospitals.

Notice how Lee photographs something ordinary, like gloves hanging up to dry, but makes it look strange and mysterious. In this photograph, it looks like the gloves are lots of loose hands.

The world around us can be confusing, worrying, scary, and unsettling. But Surrealism can encourage us to look to our imagination and dreams – they are powerful tools. You can invent new worlds (where cats have hat-like clouds above them!). You can portray yourself and the people in your lives through all sorts of symbols. Nothing needs to be as it really is.

SPOTLIGHT: FRIDA KAHLO

'I PAINT MYSELF BECAUSE I AM SO OFTEN ALONE AND BECAUSE I AM THE SUBJECT I KNOW BEST.'

There are some artists who are impossible to put into categories, and **FRIDA KAHLO** is one of them. To me, she is one of the bravest artists who has ever lived.

Little Frida Kahlo was born near Mexico City in 1907, and grew up in a house called La Casa Azul, which means 'the blue house'. She was the fourth out of five children, and her love of art came from her father, who was a photographer.

Frida and her father were very close. They both shared a curiosity for art and knowledge, but also suffered from medical conditions. At the age of six, Frida caught polio, a disease that left her with one leg shorter than the other. This meant that for nine months she was confined to her bedroom, where she spent her time thinking up imaginary friends.

When she returned to school, Frida was a hard-working student who dreamed of becoming a doctor. But at age 18, she was involved in a terrible bus crash. She was badly hurt and, under doctor's orders, had to lie in bed for three months.

So, Frida's mother installed a mirror above her bed and gave her some paints. She started by decorating her plaster casts with butterflies, but soon after began drawing herself.

In her art, Frida wasn't afraid to show how she was really feeling. We all experience many emotions in life, the good ones and the bad ones, and it shows a person's strength to be honest about this.

This painting shows Frida twice, connected by two hearts. Why do you think she's presented herself this way? It makes me think about all the different people we can be, in different situations. It also reminds me that even when we feel lonely, we still have ourselves and our imaginations to keep us company.

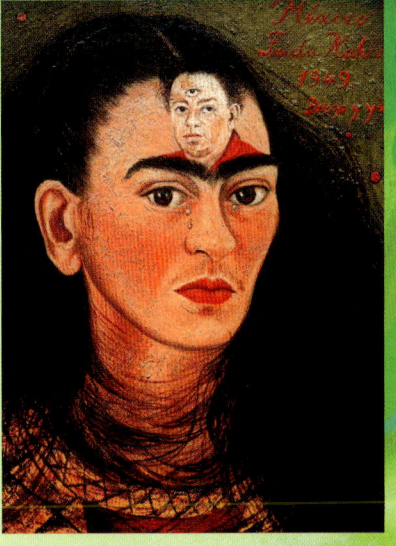

FRIDA KAHLO, *DIEGO AND I*, 1949.

Here, she has painted herself crying. But look at how she paints tears: like little crystals! Frida saw beauty in everything.

FRIDA KAHLO, *THE TWO FRIDAS*, 1939.

Frida's beautiful paintings also show how much she loved life, her friendships, nature and animals – she even kept pet monkeys at La Casa Azul! As she said:

'THERE IS NOTHING MORE PRECIOUS THAN LAUGHTER – IT IS STRENGTH TO LAUGH AND LOSE ONESELF, TO BE LIGHT.'

FRIDA KAHLO, *SELF-PORTRAIT WITH THORN NECKLACE AND HUMMINGBIRD*, 1940.

THE HARLEM RENAISSANCE

At the top of Manhattan, in New York City, is a neighbourhood called Harlem. If you visit today you'll see it's filled with bustling jazz clubs, museums and dance schools. This is because, a hundred years ago, in the 1920s and 1930s, it became home to a movement trailblazed by Black artists, dancers, poets and more. This movement, which celebrated Black culture, was known as the **HARLEM RENAISSANCE**.

Notice how the word renaissance is used? Just as we learned in the first chapter, renaissance here means 'rebirth' or 'revival'.

The Harlem Renaissance emerged at a transformative time for Black people in the United States. Slavery had been abolished in 1865. But Black communities were still kept separate from white people, and prohibited from schools, parks, universities and public spaces. Laws that enforced this discrimination in the United States were known as the Jim Crow laws (you can learn more about them on page 112), and they meant Black people had fewer opportunities and a lower quality of life. These laws existed from 1865 and lasted for about a hundred years.

SLAVERY

Slavery is when a person has ownership of another person (the 'enslaved'), by law. Enslaved people had very few rights and were forced to do back-breaking work. They were treated brutally and lived in terrible conditions. From the 1600s to the end of the American Civil War in 1865, white people enslaved mostly Black people from Africa, or descendants of Africans.

Things started to change with the **GREAT MIGRATION**. Beginning in 1910 and until around 1970, six million Black people moved from the rural South to mostly northern cities across the USA, such as New York City and Detroit (where there was less overt discrimination and better opportunities for work). As a result, new communities formed within these cities, and Harlem was one of them. By the 1920s, it was home to nearly 200,000 Black Americans, who flourished creatively.

Sculptor **META VAUX WARRICK FULLER** was one of the movement's trailblazers. She was born in Philadelphia, USA in 1877 and studied in Paris in her twenties. After meeting people associated with the Harlem Renaissance she was inspired to focus on Black life in her art.

In 1921 she sculpted *Ethiopia*, a statue of a tall, elegant, mummified figure, who is shown here 'waking up' to a dawn of greatness for Black people. Meta said about the sculpture:

'Here was a group who had once made history and now after a long sleep was awaking, gradually unwinding the bandage of its mummied past and looking out on life again, expectant but unafraid and with at least a graceful gesture.'

META VAUX WARRICK FULLER, *ETHIOPIA*, 1921.

AUGUSTA SAVAGE was born in 1892 in Florida, USA, and arrived in New York City in 1921 with just $4.60 in her pocket. She had big dreams of becoming an artist. In Harlem, she sculpted elegant **PORTRAIT BUSTS** of people in her community, such as her student, the artist **GWENDOLYN KNIGHT**.

Augusta couldn't afford to use bronze for her busts, so she worked in plaster, and added shoe polish to achieve a bronze effect. She showed that beautiful things don't have to be expensive.

PORTRAIT BUST
A portrait bust is a sculpture of someone's upper body (their head, shoulders and chest).

AUGUSTA SAVAGE, *GWENDOLYN KNIGHT*, 1934-35.

In 1939, the World's Fair asked Augusta to make a sculpture reflecting her community's musical contributions. The World's Fair renamed it *The Harp*, but its original title was *Lift Every Voice and Sing*. This referenced the hymn of the same name that, through its lyrics, inspires and reflects the hope, resilience and faith of Black American people.

AUGUSTA SAVAGE, *THE HARP*, 1939.

THE WORLD'S FAIR
The World's Fair was an important exhibition in New York City that brought together the achievements of art, science and culture from different nations across the globe.

Augusta sculpted a choir of singers draped in pleated gowns, in the shape of a harp. To the right of the sculpture, it's as if the choir is being held in the palm of a hand. Perhaps this is meant to show how singing in harmony with others brings people together.

The sculpture measured a staggering 4.8 metres in height (just smaller than a giraffe) and was placed in the middle of the fair, earning Augusta fame and praise. But after the fair ended, Augusta didn't have enough money to store it safely, and the work was destroyed.

Lack of money is something that has impacted women, especially Black women, throughout history. It's meant that we've lost, and overlooked, so much of their work. Can you imagine the positive effect a giant work such as this would have in the world if it hadn't been destroyed?

Have you ever heard of **SELMA BURKE**? No? Well, have you ever looked carefully at the US dime? You might be more familiar with Selma than you think. Born in 1900 in North Carolina, USA, Selma spent her childhood making little figurines from clay.

She began her career as a nurse but soon swapped that for art. In Harlem, she was mentored by Augusta Savage, and thrived as a sculptor. In 1943, she won a competition to sculpt a bronze relief of the then US President, Franklin D. Roosevelt. To capture his likeness, she initially sketched him from life.

SELMA BURKE, *FRANKLIN D. ROOSEVELT*, 1945.

RELIEF SCULPTURE

A relief sculpture is when the subject is slightly raised from a solid background (such as an image on a coin).

However, as Roosevelt died in 1945, he never got to see Selma's creation. Because of his death, another engraving – this time by John Sinnock – was made for the 1946 US dime. This engraving was strikingly similar to Selma's.

She was rightly outraged at the similarity and demanded that the FBI investigate. Unsurprisingly, they did not, and Sinnock never gave her credit. I strongly agree with those who say Selma should be celebrated for this artwork, and that John Sinnock's initials on the dime should be replaced by hers: 'S. B.'. The debate continues today.

Born in Boston, USA in 1905, **LOIS MAILOU JONES** (famous for painting with a little cat on her shoulder!) said that Paris offered her freedom from racial prejudices, which is the term for when people hold negative beliefs about others based on their race. Here she painted landscapes in an expressive style, but also African masks, which were a an important influence for European artists working in the early 1900s. Lois used electric shades of colouring and bold shapes for her pictures.

LOIS MAILOU JONES PAINTING IN HER PARIS STUDIO, c.1937/1938, WITH HER CAT. PHOTO BY MARC VAUX.

LOIS MAILOU JONES, *LES FÉTICHES*, 1938.

Many of these women were overlooked in their lifetimes and, for a lot of them, it is only in the last few years that their work has been properly honoured. To me, these are some of the most groundbreaking and beautiful works in history.

NEW LANDSCAPES: BRAZIL AND THE UNITED STATES

Where do you live? In a flat, or in a house? On a street in a bustling town, or on a remote lane in the countryside? High up in the mountains, or by the sea?

When an artist depicts a place – whether it's where they live, or somewhere they like to visit – they don't have to make it look realistic. They can play around with what that place looks and feels like.

If it's hot, they might show the heat through warm colours. Or if it's cold, they could use frosty blues and sharp, icy edges. They might think about how to capture noises, like the humming of crickets or people playing music. But they may also choose to express a place's history, and the stories its people tell.

At the start of the twentieth century, many artists captured where they lived in new ways. This was happening a lot around the world because of big changes that were going on at that time. Around four hundred years before this, in the sixteenth century, European countries (including Britain, Portugal and Spain) had invaded other countries across the world. They claimed rule over these countries and the people who lived in them, often with terrible violence. This was known as **COLONIZING**, or **COLONIALIZATION**.

The European colonizers also brought with them their own ideas of art and architecture. This often meant the country's cultural identity was ignored and erased. Colonization caused huge amounts of disruption, misery and the death of millions of people. It has also shaped these countries in ways that are still felt today.

> If you find yourself in colonized countries outside Europe, you will notice that some of the architecture will be in a 'colonial' style (with features such as columns and symmetrical windows). Colonizers often renamed places, too. For example, the British named one of the American colonies 'New England'.

As the centuries progressed, these countries started to gain independence from their colonizers. This was often achieved with great struggle, many battles, and through the actions of brave people.

In 1822, Brazil started a years-long war to gain independence from its colonizer, Portugal. In 1922, to mark the 100th anniversary of the start of the war, the people of Brazil created a year of celebration. Among other events was the Semana de Arte Moderno ('Modern Art Week'), a festival in São Paulo staged by a group of artists. It was an exciting time, and artists, poets and musicians began to ask themselves: *How can we celebrate our country through art?*

TARSILA DO AMARAL, FAVELLA HILL, 1924.

For centuries, previously colonized countries, like Brazil, had adopted European styles of art, and we have looked at many of these in earlier chapters. But in 1920s Brazil, artists wanted to invent a new national identity.

TARSILA DO AMARAL was born in São Paulo, Brazil in 1886. As a young woman, she went to study art in Paris, but she often found herself thinking about where she came from.

Following her studies, she travelled around Brazil searching for inspiration to use in her work. She looked at native plants, trees and animals, the bright blue sky and the favelas (where communities lived on the outskirts of cities). You can see this in *Favella Hill*.

Tarsila also wanted to include images of carnival in her work. Carnival is an annual festival that happens in many places around the world but celebrated with special gusto in Brazil, to celebrate Brazilian heritage and culture. It's full of costumes, parades, music and dancing.

> In **CARNIVAL IN MADUREIRA**, 1924, Tarsila paints people of all ages dressed for carnival. When I look at this painting, I feel like I can hear the sounds of people chatting, and the guitar and drums playing offbeat rhythms in a Brazilian musical style called Samba. What sounds do you hear when you look at this painting?

TARSILA DO AMARAL, *CARNIVAL IN MADUREIRA*, 1924.

> Do you notice how Tarsila has also included that large, industrial tower? As well as showing Brazilian culture, she's also thinking about how modern structures were transforming the landscape.

In North America around the same time, an artist called **GEORGIA O'KEEFFE** was also making art to represent where she lived. While Georgia and Tarsila were working in very different circumstances, both artists showed how the landscapes around them were changing rapidly in the twentieth century, as new towers and skyscrapers were built.

Born in 1887 in Wisconsin, USA, Georgia grew up on a farm. At the age of 12, she announced she was going to be an artist, and after her studies became an art teacher. In 1918, she moved to New York City to pursue her dreams to be a full-time artist. Here, she painted many things, including towering skyscrapers, often at night with windows lit from within. You can imagine her marvelling at these buildings, the speed of the city, and the wonder of this whole new world.

Georgia once said:

'ONE CAN'T PAINT NEW YORK AS IT IS, BUT RATHER AS IT IS FELT.'

GEORGIA O'KEEFFE, *RADIATOR BUILDING—NIGHT, NEW YORK*, 1927.

When I look at **RADIATOR BUILDING—NIGHT, NEW YORK**, 1927, it transports me to the city. You can see plumes of smoke and strobes of light bouncing off the buildings, creating a sense of excitement.

But Georgia also loved nature. After spending summers in the New Mexico desert in the south-west of the USA, she moved there permanently in the 1940s. Swapping the blacks and greys of New York for blazes of reds, oranges and blues in New Mexico, Georgia made art that showed what it felt like to live in a place where the skies are vast, and the sunlight intense.

> In **BLACK MESA LANDSCAPE**, 1930, she shows us how varied the landscape can be. At the bottom we see lush green trees; in the middle are dry, dusty cliffs with veinlike lines; and at the top are whites and blues for the soft, icy mountain peaks. It's very different to New York City, don't you think?

GEORGIA O'KEEFFE, *BLACK MESA LANDSCAPE, NEW MEXICO*, 1930.

ART TASK

Wherever you live, you can depict it in a piece of art. What shapes and colours would you use to show the landscape? How will you show the feeling or history of the place? Why not step outside, find some inspiration and see what you can create!

ABSTRACT EXPRESSIONISM

In the 1940s and 1950s, a group of artist friends were living amid the busyness of downtown New York City. Having survived the **GREAT DEPRESSION** and the Second World War, here they found themselves in a whole new world – with new music and new art.

THE GREAT DEPRESSION

The Great Depression was a ten-year long period, starting in 1929, when terrible economic conditions made life very hard for people. It started in the United States, but soon spread across the world. Many people lost their money and jobs, and faced hunger and homelessness.

So how could they use their art to reflect these changes, and express their feelings? Some artists took their paintings off the easel and placed them on the floor to work. Others poured, dripped and swirled paint on their (at times, gigantic) canvases, rather than using traditional brushstrokes. Some used their whole bodies to create sweeping shapes and lines, which, as we learned on page 62, makes an abstract image.

CANVAS

A canvas is a strong cloth that is stretched to make the surface of a painting.

These artists worked in these ways to 'express' themselves. This led to a whole new movement, called **ABSTRACT EXPRESSIONISM.**

LEE KRASNER was at the centre of this movement. She was born in Brooklyn, USA, in 1908, and as a young girl was fiercely independent. Enchanted by the painters working in Paris at the start of the 1900s, Lee had her eyes opened when she visited the Museum of Modern Art (MoMA). Founded in New York in 1929, this was the first museum in the United States dedicated entirely to modern art. Lee said that seeing these works was so dazzling, it was like a 'bomb that exploded'.

LEE KRASNER, *THE SEASONS*, 1957.

> Lee called this painting **THE SEASONS**, 1957. It's made up of giant swathes of colour and looks like a cycle of leaf and flower shapes that continuously grow and decay. It reminds me of the seasons, which come and go, year after year. But it also makes me think about the different feelings and experiences that come and go throughout our lives. What do you see?

Viewing an artwork in person is so different to seeing it in a book. If you can, try and take a trip to a museum to witness the textures, colours and splendours of art up close.

I've seen this painting in person. It's ginormous, measuring over 5 metres wide – that's over three park benches long! When you're in front of it, it completely takes you over, as all you can see are explosions of paint wherever you look.

JOAN MITCHELL, born in 1925 in Chicago, USA, was in Lee's wider friendship circle and also made expressive paintings. She liked to squeeze thick lines of paint straight from the tube onto the canvas. If you look to the side of Joan's paintings in real life, you can see how thickly she applied her paint.

She was known as an 'action painter', and you can almost feel her attacking the canvas with her giant brushes – which were usually reserved for industrial-sized projects!

> Clearly, Joan is expressing a lot of feelings here. The blue perhaps shows some sadness to her art, whilst the bright oranges might remind us that light and happiness are around the corner.

JOAN MITCHELL, *WEEDS*, 1976.

Like many artists throughout history, Lee and Joan were great friends with writers and poets. Together, they made up what's called an **ARTISTIC COMMUNITY**: creatives who inspire and help each other, and who sometimes work together on projects, too. Joan liked to work with poets and capture their words through colour. For this she used pastel.

PASTEL
Pastel is a powdery crayon. It can be effective for creating different shades of the same colour.

The image below features a poem written in 1975 by Joan's friend James Schuyler, called 'Daylight'. It reads:

AND WHEN I THOUGHT,
"OUR LOVE MIGHT END"
THE SUN
WENT RIGHT ON SHINING

JOAN MITCHELL, *DAYLIGHT*, c. 1975.

What do you think this means? I think it speaks to how love is endless, just like the sun, that continues to shine, day after day.

ART TASK

Why don't you try drawing your favourite poem? What might the words look like? Or you could get a friend to write a poem, and together think about what colours you might use to capture it.

I love Abstract Expressionism for its power to express different emotions and possibilities, which viewers can interpret for themselves.

These artists were instrumental in making New York City the new art capital of the Western world. Like Paris in the early 1900s, it became home to artists who would go on to spark all sorts of new styles and movements – which you'll learn more about in the next chapters.

A NEW TYPE OF ART: EXPERIMENTATION

Between 1939 and 1945, millions of people fought in the Second World War, which began in Europe, and soon involved Africa, Asia, the Soviet Union and the United States. It was more violent and bloody than the First World War, with even more people killed and wounded.

Around the world, towns and communities were destroyed, food supplies were at an all-time low, and lots of children were moved to the countryside, or even another country, to keep them safe.

In Japan, the destruction was especially huge. In the summer of 1945, the United States dropped a new type of bomb on two Japanese cities – first Hiroshima and then Nagasaki. This was an atomic bomb, which was much more powerful. These bombs caused thousands of immediate deaths, plus much ongoing damage to people's health. This violent event, however, ultimately led to the end of the war.

YOKO ONO was 12 years old in 1945. Before the war ended, she was evacuated to the countryside for safety with her brother, Keisuke. The pair travelled with very few belongings, and so they turned to that one tool we always carry with us: imagination.

At a time when food was scarce, the siblings invented a game where they dreamed up the tastiest foods and 'swapped imaginary menus in the air'. Yoko described this as her 'first piece of art'. From then on, she continued to use her mind and body as a way of making art. Without access to materials like paints or paper, she learned to use what was available to her.

Lots of artists working at the same time as Yoko found themselves in a similar situation. This led to the creation of **PERFORMANCE ART**. No longer did art have to be something stuck to a wall, or confined to an object. Now it could be something performed.

Take, for example, a work Yoko started in 1996 and which continues to this day: her *Wish Tree*. In places all over the world, she plants trees and provides viewers with a piece of paper, string, a pen and an instruction.

'MAKE A WISH. WRITE IT DOWN ON A PIECE OF PAPER. FOLD IT AND TIE IT AROUND A BRANCH OF A WISH TREE. ASK YOUR FRIENDS TO DO THE SAME. KEEP WISHING UNTIL THE BRANCHES ARE COVERED WITH WISHES.'

ART TASK

Yoko's *Wish Tree* shows that we can come together to create something beautiful, peaceful and hopeful. And that art can belong anywhere – even in your garden, local park or school. Why don't you try writing down a wish, hanging it on a tree, and starting a new wish tree near you?

GUTAI

In the late 1940s and 1950s, Japan was slowly recovering and rebuilding. During the war, Japanese artists had been under strict instruction to only make works that celebrated the military and the war. Artists, now finally free to create art without restrictions, began to experiment with new ways of expressing themselves. Some took things to new, electrical heights!

ATSUKO TANAKA, born in Osaka, Japan, in 1932, was one of the few women in a group of artists who called themselves the **GUTAI ART ASSOCIATION**. The group's mission was to make experimental art and 'create what has never been done before'. So, prioritizing playfulness, they poured paint on to the wheels of their bikes and then rode over sheets of paper. Or they smashed bottles filled with paint on to a canvas, resulting in paintings full of dripping lines and excitingly messy shapes.

Maybe check with your teachers or parents before you try experimenting like the Gutai...

In 1956, at the opening night of the second Gutai Art Exhibition in Tokyo, Atsuko exhibited ... herself! She used her body as art, dressing up almost like a living sculpture. She covered herself with around two hundred hand-painted lightbulbs, flashing and twinkling in reds, greens, yellows and blues.

ATSUKO TANAKA, *ELECTRIC DRESS*, 1956.

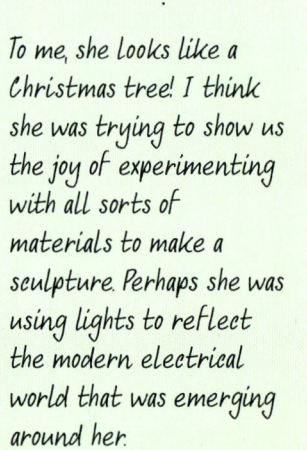

To me, she looks like a Christmas tree! I think she was trying to show us the joy of experimenting with all sorts of materials to make a sculpture. Perhaps she was using lights to reflect the modern electrical world that was emerging around her.

BLACK MOUNTAIN COLLEGE

As experimentation soared, schools that worked with this new style and approach began to open. One of these was Black Mountain College, set in rural North Carolina, in the USA. The forward-thinking school was founded in 1933 and made sure that art was at the centre of its syllabus. It also promoted equality between teachers and students, and all genders and races, which was radical for the time.

Among the teaching staff at the school were a German couple, the artists **ANNI ALBERS** and Josef Albers. Anni made bold, patterned textiles, full of jazzy textures and bright colours. She encouraged her students 'to learn through doing' (which essentially means working things out as you go along!).

She also taught her students to use the resources that they had around them, like everyday objects you can find in your home, such as string or paper clips.

ANNI ALBERS, *BLACK-WHITE-YELLOW*, ORIGINAL 1926 (LOST), REWOVEN BY GUNTA STÖLZL, 1965.

One of the star pupils at Black Mountain was **RUTH ASAWA**. She was born in 1926 to Japanese parents, and brought up on a farm in California, USA, where she often made small sculptures and bracelets out of wire recycled from vegetable crates.

She began her studies at Black Mountain at the age of 20, where she thrived in its experimental environment. But it was on her summer break, when she travelled to Mexico, that she learned the art of basketmaking. She used this new knowledge to develop her own technique of making sculptures from wire.

Inspired by the shapes we see in nature – from the curves of leaves to the roots of trees – she looped the wires in all different directions and hung them from the ceiling.

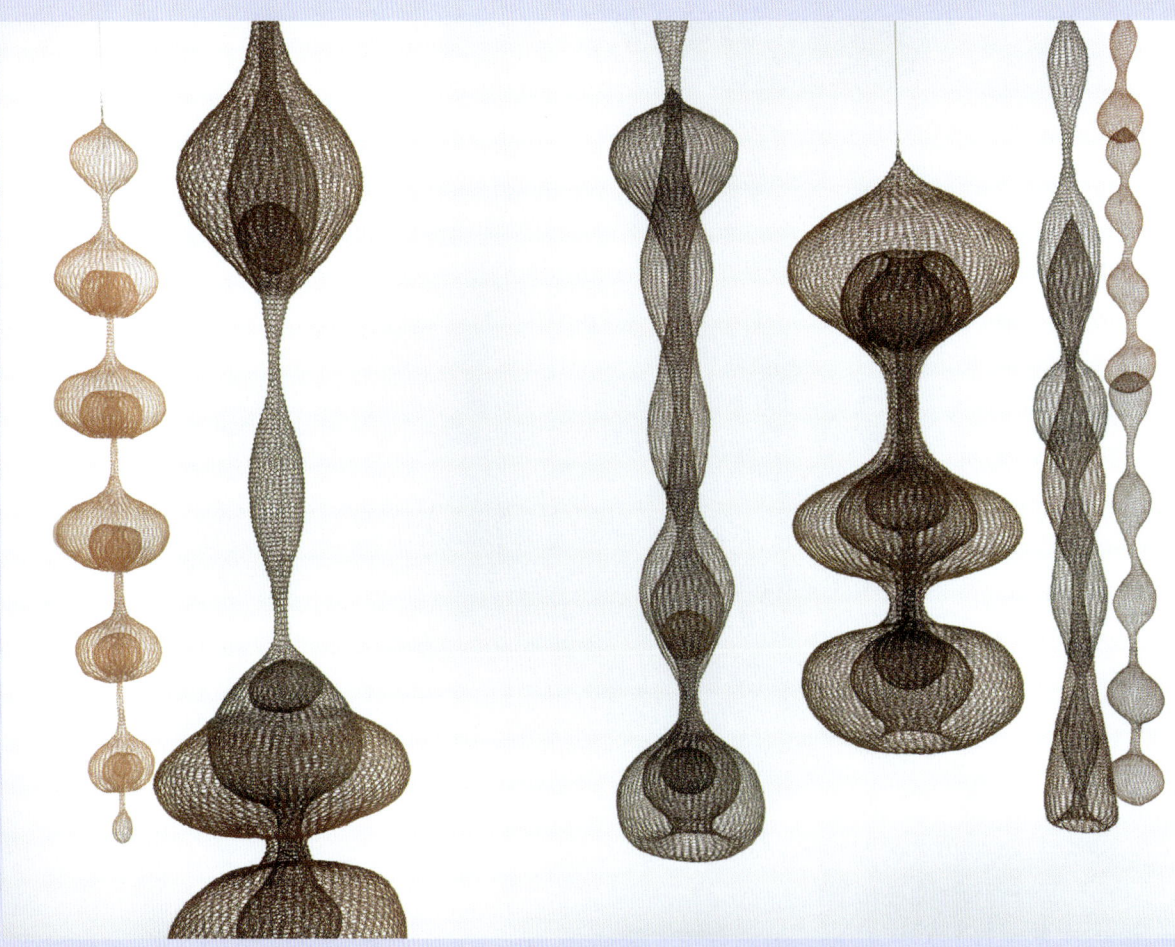

INSTALLATION VIEW OF *RUTH ASAWA: LIFE'S WORK* AT THE PULITZER ARTS FOUNDATION, ST LOUIS, 2018-19.

Look closely at her work. Do the continuous loops of her sculptures remind you of anything in nature? To me, their round shapes resemble a cocoon!

After her studies, in 1949, Ruth moved to San Francisco (where she also raised her six children). But she always carried the 'spirit' of Black Mountain College with her, caring deeply about equality, community and arts education for all.

She wanted to show that you don't need expensive materials to make art. So, in the late 1960s, she set up art workshops across San Francisco's schools, providing children of all backgrounds with cheap materials – such as flour, salt and water – to make art. Once moulded and then baked in the oven, these materials hardened to become sculptures, which Ruth sometimes cast into bronze!

'ART WILL MAKE PEOPLE BETTER, MORE HIGHLY SKILLED IN THINKING AND IMPROVING WHATEVER BUSINESS ONE GOES INTO, OR WHATEVER OCCUPATION. IT MAKES A PERSON BROADER . . .'
– RUTH ASAWA

Ruth believed in the power of art, especially experimental art, as it requires so much creativity and imagination. She understood that these skills can be applied to many different areas of our lives.

MINIMALISM

Have you ever stared at a painting full of dots, lines or simple shapes, and wondered: *What's all the fuss about?*

In the chapter on Abstract Expressionism (page 88), we looked at paintings filled with action and emotion, where the artist had clearly attacked the canvas with a paintbrush. But in the late 1950s and early 1960s, artists began reacting against this movement. They created a new style that was all about straight lines and sharp angles, with little colour and 'minimal' expression. This was known as **MINIMALISM**.

MINIMALISM
Minimalism is a style characterized by simple shapes and repetitive marks. Minimalist paintings often take the form of a 'grid' (like your maths workbooks), and sculptures could be cubes or cuboids.

ART TASK
Go to a gallery and stand in front of a Minimalist artwork, or look at a picture of one in a book or online for a while. You might find that you have more of a reaction to it than you expect. It might be calming, or perhaps make you feel dizzy!

The artists I am about to show you weren't typical Minimalist artists, but their art grew out of this tradition. This is because in the 1950s and 1960s, Minimalism was dominated by male artists, and women were often left out of many of the key exhibitions. But, as we will see, they took the style and made it their own, in the most wondrous and imaginative ways.

Let's start with the 'princess of polka dots', **YAYOI KUSAMA**. Yayoi was born in Japan in 1929. Around the age of ten, she began to experience visions, where dots and flowers appeared before her eyes. Yayoi found these visions scary, and to help her through them, she turned to art.

'I FIGHT PAIN, ANXIETY, AND FEAR EVERY DAY, AND THE ONLY METHOD I HAVE FOUND THAT RELIEVES MY ILLNESS IS TO KEEP CREATING ART.'

When she was in her twenties, Yayoi was determined to be a famous artist. She wrote a letter to her hero, Georgia O'Keeffe (page 86), who wrote back advising Yayoi on how to become an artist in New York. Yayoi travelled to the US, settling in New York, alongside artists working in **MINIMALISM**. She played with this style and made art inspired by her visions. She titled some of her paintings Infinity Nets.

From far away, these paintings might just look like a grey-ish rectangle. But look closer and you'll see scoops and licks of white paint that make up a continuous pattern of dots – too many to possibly count! Have a think about the title too... Looking at the painting is a bit like being caught in a net, don't you think?

YAYOI KUSAMA, *INFINITY NETS (1)*, 1958.

> This is a close-up of Yayoi's infinity nets.

> See how Yayoi is using the repetitive marks found in Minimalist art.

YAYOI KUSAMA AT WORK, 2013.

Yayoi then turned her hand to sculpture, making giant dotty pumpkins! This bright yellow one, made out of resin and metal, lives outdoors on an island called Naoshima in Japan. Incredibly, Naoshima is an island dedicated exclusively to art! About 3,000 people live on the island. There are a few hotels and houses across its three villages, but its main attractions are Yayoi's pumpkin and the art museums. It sounds like my dream holiday destination!

YAYOI KUSAMA, *PUMPKIN*, 1994, IN NAOSHIMA, JAPAN.

> Yayoi has created lots of other pumpkins in a whole range of sizes, colours, materials and patterns.

Next, Yayoi created rooms for people to step into, filled with thousands of lights flickering in all different colours. With mirrors on every wall and across the ceiling, the lights seem to go on forever. She called these her **INFINITY MIRROR ROOMS**, and they help viewers understand what her dot-filled visions feel like.

I've been lucky enough to experience one of these rooms. It's the closest thing I've ever felt to being up in space, surrounded by galaxies and the Milky Way!

YAYOI KUSAMA, *INFINITY MIRRORED ROOM – THE SOULS OF MILLIONS OF LIGHT YEARS AWAY*, INSTALLATION AT DAVID ZWIRNER GALLERY, NEW YORK, 2013.

YAYOI KUSAMA IN HER ROOM INSTALLATION, *GUIDEPOST TO THE NEW SPACE*, JAPAN, 2012.

Yayoi wears dots, too! This is her in a dotty dress, surrounded by her dotty paintings.

ALMA THOMAS was born in 1891, and lived most of her life in Washington D.C. She was painting at a time when rockets were blasting off the Earth at stratospheric speed. No one had ever seen anything like it before, and it was particularly exciting because people were able to watch this space mission on their newly invented colour televisions! Alma wanted to capture this groundbreaking moment through paint.

In **BLAST OFF**, 1970, Alma shows a rocket shooting off into the multicoloured sky. Look at how she captures the fiery moment, using a triangle of orange fire much bigger than the thin strip of yellow (the rocket).

ALMA THOMAS, BLAST OFF, 1970.

Did you notice how Alma has used repetitive blocks of colour to create her picture? Have you ever watched a video of a rocket taking off? Because of the heat from the fire and gas, the air around the rocket blurs. Alma's painting style allows her to depict both this blurriness and the speed of the fast-moving rocket.

ART TASK
Why don't you try drawing a scene through dots of colour and see what you can create?

For most of Alma's life, she worked as a high school teacher. It was only after she retired, aged 69, that she was able to focus on her art career full-time. Within a few years, she was sharing her art in exhibitions and receiving great praise and recognition. She became the first Black woman to have a solo exhibition at the Whitney Museum of American Art (one of the most important museums in the world).

When I was younger, my favourite artist was **BRIDGET RILEY**. She was born in London in 1931 and painted pictures that totally discombobulated (confused) my vision. Her paintings give the effect of **OPTICAL ILLUSIONS**.

She worked in a style known as **OP ART**, short for Optical Art. It has a strange effect on your vision, as the images appear to move, blur or change.

> **OPTICAL ILLUSION**
> An optical illusion tricks your eyes into thinking you're seeing something that's not actually there.

Bridget grew up in London, but the outbreak of the Second World War meant she had to escape to safety in Cornwall, on the far south-western coast of England. The dramatic rocky and hilly landscape and the waves of Cornwall's sea always remained an inspiration to her. In her paintings she captures all the colours of the sea, glittering in the sunlight, along with the constant motion of slowly rolling waves.

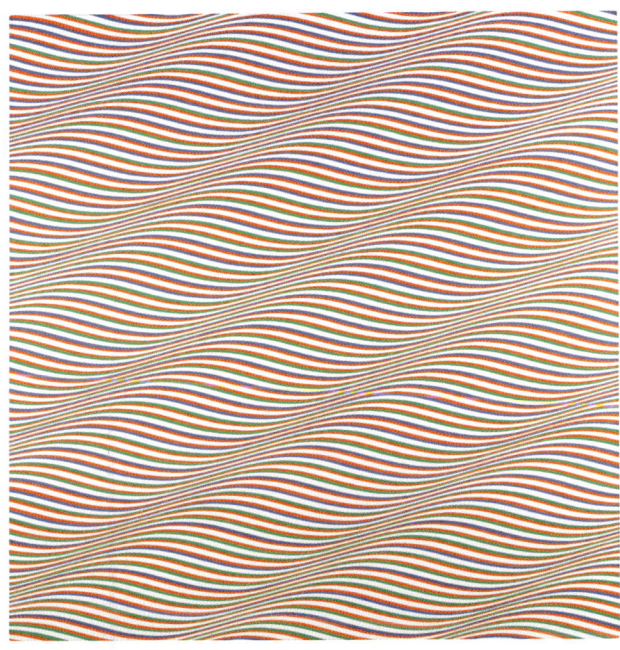

BRIDGET RILEY, GALA, 1974.

> Isn't it extraordinary how these paintings, which are made of just a few shapes and lines, can get us to imagine all sorts of things? And if you look long enough, it seems like the painting begins to move...

The poet and painter **ETEL ADNAN** was born in Beirut, Lebanon in 1925. She lived all around the world, including Paris and California, and could speak many languages. Her paintings consisted of simple shapes in bright colours, and what you see can change depending on how you choose to look at them.

ETEL ADNAN, UNTITLED, 2014.

> What do you see? I see a sun setting on the horizon line, behind a thin strip of blue. But the sun isn't green, and the sky is rarely yellow, so you might see something different. Maybe the other sun reflecting upside down on the water!

POP ART

What sparks to mind when you think of 'pop'? Pop culture? Pop music? Pop stars? Or something that goes pop – like popcorn? This was exactly what artists in Europe and the United States were asking in the 1950s and 1960s.

Just like the fashions of the day (when women began to wear bright patterns and short skirts and had sleek, short bobs as haircuts), **POP ARTISTS** worked with bold colours and simple shapes. They looked to comic books, film stars, advertisements and famous logos (like Coca-Cola) for artistic inspiration, and were all about capturing something 'popular'!

SISTER MARY CORITA (CORITA KENT), the Hollywood-based former nun and educator, even found inspiration in the supermarket. Her art was all about spreading faith and love, and seeing beauty in the world. In the 1960s, she used the colours and dots in the logo for Wonder Bread (an American bread company) to get us to see the 'wonder' in bread.

Think about all the ways food can enrich and nourish us, helping us to grow. Bread is a food enjoyed by people all over the world, and to 'break bread' is to share a meal with our friends.

SISTER MARY CORITA, ENRICHED BREAD, 1965.

Sister Corita wanted her work to be affordable and widely available. So, she and other Pop artists used a technique called **SCREEN PRINTING**, where many copies of the same work could be easily made, without complicated machinery.

Over in England, **PAULINE BOTY** was fast becoming the star of British Pop art. Born in London in 1938, Pauline acted in films, often appeared on the radio and, when it came to art, she painted the celebrities of the day. She said they were 'present-day mythology' – ancient Greek gods and goddesses for the modern world.

ART TASK
Do you have any favourite singers or actors? Have a go at drawing them, to create your very own Pop art image...

Her 1963 painting *The Only Blonde in the World* features the film star Marilyn Monroe.

Pauline has painted Marilyn shimmering in a silver dress. I love that she's also painted her with the sun reflecting off her tassels and sequins, bathing her in light and making her appear almost like a statue.

PAULINE BOTY, *THE ONLY BLONDE IN THE WORLD*, 1963.

Look at how she's also framed Marilyn between two green panels, perhaps opening to show us the glamour of Hollywood. But it also reminds me of when the curtains close at the theatre or cinema. By painting this last glimpse of her hero, who died the year before this painting was made, Pauline seems to be wanting Marilyn to last forever, even as the credits roll.

This was, after all, the era of a new phenomenon: colour television. Before this, screens used to be black and white (can you imagine!?), but colour TVs became popular in the late 1960s, and were normal by the 1980s. Artists were amazed and awestruck by technicolour screens, and injected this luminosity into their art.

EVELYNE AXELL went by her surname, 'Axell'. She was born in Belgium in 1935, and was fanatical about colour.

This is her painting of a girl licking an ice cream. Look at the clever way Axell has used bright colours to visualize the sweet, zingy taste. Notice how the girl's face is in black and white and her eyes are closed, like she is in a dreamlike state.

EVELYNE AXELL, ICE CREAM 1, 1964.

Think about when you last tried something sweet. It can feel like your taste buds are alive with colour!

But Axell didn't stop there. To make her work even more 'Pop', she added real-life objects to her canvas that could be bought from a shop – like this painting, **VALENTINE**, from 1966. Here she has painted a silhouette of a woman with a typical 1960s hairdo, beside a toy-size space helmet. It is a work that honours Valentina Tereshkova, an engineer and cosmonaut and the only woman to have ever undertaken a solo space mission.

By painting her subject against a glittering gold backdrop, Axell shows that a woman can be both glamorous and achieve their dreams (in this case, of travelling into space!).

EVELYNE AXELL, *VALENTINE*, 1966.

Why do you think Axell has added a toy-size helmet, instead of a real one? Perhaps this demonstrates the struggle women faced to be taken seriously in the space profession?

Sadly, it was hard for women to be taken seriously in lots of different professions. It didn't help that advertising back then often portrayed women as obsessed only with shopping and clothes, never thinking about anything else.

Artists of the time looked carefully at how women were being portrayed in advertising. The Venezuelan artist **MARISOL ESCOBAR** (who went by just 'Marisol') had fun with this. Born in 1930 in Paris, she grew up in Europe and America. While working in New York in the 1960s, she understood how ridiculous these adverts were. For her work *Dinner Date*, she hand-carved sculptures of two almost identical women, dressed in the fanciest fashions of the day and looking bored out of their minds.

ADVERTISEMENT FOR WAYENBERG MASSAGIC SHOES, 1972.

MARISOL, *DINNER DATE*, 1963.

No one would ever want to be as blank-faced and boxed-in as these women, even though they wore fashionable clothes and dined in style. So, Marisol was using the power of art to show us how women were silenced and belittled, while also being used to sell clothes and experiences. But she also understood the power of humour and, by turning something into 'art', she challenges us to look at a situation differently.

That's what Pop artists did: they showed us another way of looking at something that was already there.

111

BLACK POWER: THE CIVIL RIGHTS MOVEMENT

Throughout the United States the cruel and dehumanizing practice of slavery was legal until 1865 (as we learned about on page 77). Most of the enslaved people were of African descent, and their treatment was often brutal.

Between 1861 and 1865, there was a civil war in the United States, finally resulting in the abolition (ending) of slavery. However, many states responded with the so-called 'Jim Crow' laws, which still kept Black people from having the same rights as white people. These included forcing them to pay extra taxes or take unnecessary tests just so they could vote. These rules were unfair and made Black people's lives extremely difficult.

In the 1950s and 1960s, Black Americans across the United States joined forces. They wanted to live their lives with the same freedoms and rights as white people. They'd had enough. So they campaigned together for equality, marching in the streets, making public speeches and protesting.

It took a whole movement to overturn these unfair laws, and this was known as the **CIVIL RIGHTS MOVEMENT**.

SOCIAL MOVEMENT

When I talk about a movement here, I'm referring to a social movement, which is when groups of people come together to create change and achieve their shared goals.

The artists associated with this movement wanted to use their art to fight for this change. They also began to think about what their art might look like in this new era. For many, it was about honouring Black people and spreading positive messages of togetherness and hope for a better and more inclusive world.

As a young girl, **ELIZABETH CATLETT**, born in 1915 in Washington D.C., grew up listening to her grandmother telling her stories about being born into slavery – and particularly about her life on the **PLANTATIONS**.

With her grandmother's stories at the front of her mind, Elizabeth dedicated her life to honouring and illustrating the beauty of Black people through her art.

'I HAVE ALWAYS WANTED MY ART TO SERVICE MY PEOPLE—TO REFLECT US, TO RELATE TO US, TO STIMULATE US, TO MAKE US AWARE OF OUR POTENTIAL.'

One of her most effective works, I think, is called *Black Unity*.

PLANTATIONS

Plantations were large farm sites in the Southern United States (and other places), where crops like cotton, tobacco or sugar were grown. Enslaved people lived on these plantations and worked from dawn until dusk, under the fierce midday sun, in terrible and violent conditions.

ELIZABETH CATLETT, *BLACK UNITY*, 1968.

This double-sided sculpture shows, on one side, a clenched fist and on the other side, two faces conjoined, perhaps demonstrating that we are stronger together.

The clenched fist has a long history as a symbol of strength and unity. For example, in the Black Power movement, it stood for resistance.

This symbol appeared in wider culture too. At the time when Elizabeth was living in Mexico, Tommie Smith and John Carlos – Black athletes representing the USA at the 1968 Olympic Games in Mexico City – took gold and bronze medals in the 200 metres. They stood on the podium with their fists clenched in the air. It was a brave and powerful statement against the oppression of Black people. Even though they were fighting for the rights they deserved, they were suspended from the Olympics and sent home.

TOMMIE SMITH AND JOHN CARLOS RAISE THE BLACK POWER SALUTE. OLYMPIC GAMES, MEXICO CITY, 1968.

The clenched fist is still used as a symbol today. It is most strongly linked to the **BLACK LIVES MATTER** movement, which seeks to highlight racism, discrimination and violence experienced by Black people.

Despite facing resistance, artists continued to fight. A few years after the 1968 Olympic games, **BARBARA JONES-HOGU**, an artist born in Chicago, USA, in 1938, made a print called *Unite (First State)*, 1969.

> With their clenched fists in the air, these activists stand below a colourful sky that has the word UNITE scattered across it. Notice how it's repeated lots of times? It's as if everyone is chanting the word 'Unite' together, showing us the strength of their collective energy – and adding a sound effect to a silent image.

BARBARA JONES-HOGU, *UNITE*, 1971.

Barbara was part of a group of artists in Chicago called AfriCOBRA. They made colourful, joyous artworks that aimed to 'preach positivity to the people'. Full of rhythm, this was a new style that was intentionally different from European painting and sculpture.

CAROLYN MIMS LAWRENCE, born in the United States in 1940, was also part of this group. She made a painting called *Black Children Keep Your Spirits Free*, in 1972. If you look closely, you can see the title is included in the painting multiple times, in lots of different colours.

CAROLYN MIMS LAWRENCE, *BLACK CHILDREN KEEP YOUR SPIRITS FREE*, 1972.

I love this work. Full of bright colour and energy, it's like you can hear the sounds of the drumming and music!

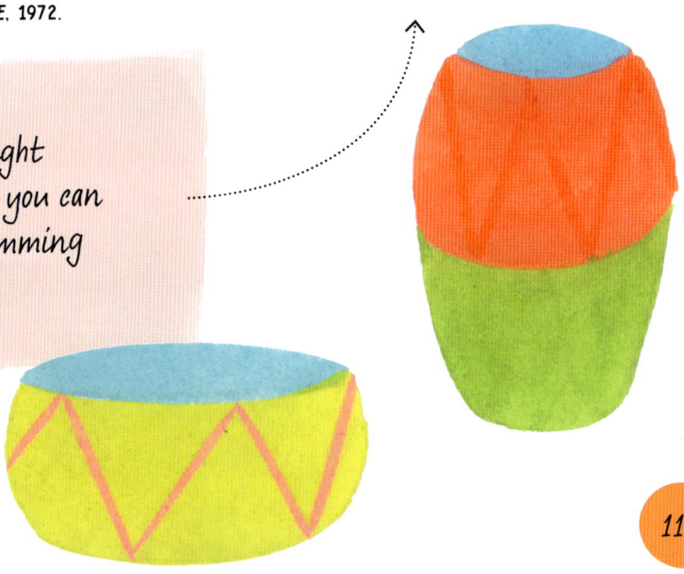

117

Artists also turned to quilt-making at this time. Why? Well, as we saw on page 38, quilts have a history of being used as a form of protest because they were one of the few art forms accessible to women. Quilt-making can also be an impactful way to tell stories, and for artists to share their personal experiences and viewpoints.

FAITH RINGGOLD, who was born in Harlem, USA in 1930, at the height of the Harlem Renaissance (see page 76), loved working with paint and fabrics. As a little girl, she suffered from bad bouts of asthma, which meant she spent a lot of time off school. Her mother, Willi Posey Jones, was a dressmaker and taught little Faith how to sew.

When she was older, Faith made painted quilts that celebrated the key leaders of the Civil Rights Movement, including Dr Martin Luther King Jr. In 1963, he gave a very famous speech now known as 'I Have a Dream'. In this, he called for a fairer world, where people are treated the same, no matter their skin colour. The speech was a landmark moment. It attracted huge crowds, uniting people across the United States, and inspiring real change. Still today, it is considered one of the greatest speeches of all time.

Ringgold captured this moment in a beautiful quilt that features a portrait of Martin Luther King Jr making his speech. He is smartly dressed, with a determined look, surrounded by a bed of pink flowers. These reference the pink roses planted in the World Peace Rose Garden in his honour, in his birth city of Atlanta, USA.

FAITH RINGGOLD, COMING TO JONES ROAD TANKA #3: MARTIN LUTHER KING, 2010.

Ringgold was so inspired by Dr Martin Luther King Jr that she later wrote a children's book about his life and the Civil Rights Movement called *My Dream of Martin Luther King*. She wanted to inspire the next generation to keep the spirit of resistance alive.

TEXTILES:
1950S TO THE PRESENT DAY

What type of art can be hard, soft, long, thin, wide, stringy or fluffy? Made to look like a waterfall, a patchwork, people or animals? Can be worn, turned into a blanket, wrapped, bundled or tied?

I think **TEXTILE ART** is the most wide-ranging of all art forms. It can include fabrics, cloth, or natural and synthetic fibres, rope, silk, satin, lace and quilts. But, despite all the inventive ways it can be used, textiles have not been taken seriously until recently – which is shocking, if you ask me!

Remember when we learned that the Royal Academy banned needlework from being included in its exhibitions? You'll recall that textile art has a history of being seen as 'women's work'. For a long time, it was the most accessible art form for women, because it could, for instance, be done in the home. Thankfully, today textiles are finally recognized as a respectable art form. But it's taken a long time, and a lot of work.

It's especially shocking when we find out all the incredible things textiles can be used for: warmth, protest (like banners), clothes, tents, hammocks, storytelling and a way of expressing oneself.

Let's go back to when artists began to take textiles to new heights. **SHEILA HICKS** was born on a farm in Nebraska, USA, in 1934.

She learned to sew, embroider and knit from her mother and grandmothers, and after learning about art and architecture at art school, Sheila began experimenting with fibre. She uses threads to create art of all sorts, from small starlike sculptures, to a ginormous cascading rainbow waterfall!

SHEILA HICKS, *PILLAR OF INQUIRY/SUPPLE COLUMN*, 2013-14.

While most art requires us to 'look' rather than 'touch', Sheila encourages us to do both. She likes us to 'feel' her sculptures, so we can understand their textures. In her own words:

'I LIKE TO SAY THAT THE KIND OF ART I CREATE CAN SOMETIMES BE DONE WITH MY EYES CLOSED, JUST BY FEELING WITH MY FINGERS.'

Tactility is a big part of textiles ('tactile' is a word that is used to describe something that is nice to touch). In fact, we surround ourselves with fibre all day. Think about what you're wearing right now. How does it feel – heavy or breezy, scratchy or smooth? This is what Sheila wants us to ask when we are with her artworks.

SHEILA HICKS, *INSTALLATION FROM "FORAY INTO CHROMATIC ZONES"*, 2015.

This is Sheila lying down on one of her fibre installations. Looks welcoming!

MRINALINI MUKHERJEE, born in Mumbai, India, in 1949, used rope to make giant imaginary characters. Some are nearly double her height! She made her animal-like figures in deep purples, yellows and browns, and twisted, folded and knotted the rope into incredible shapes.

To me, her sculptures look like ancient gods who once ruled the world.

MRINALINI MUKHERJEE WITH *WOMAN ON A SWING*, 1989.

Poet and artist **CECILIA VICUÑA**, who was born in Santiago, Chile, in 1948, creates giant forests of threads. She uses a technique called **QUIPU** to honour the Quecha people, a community in the Andes who, thousands of years ago, used this technique to communicate.

They hand-tied knots and, depending on the colour, order and number of them, the knots meant different things. The Quechua people used them to keep records and send messages.

QUIPU, c. 1400–1532.

But when the Spanish conquered the Inca Empire in the sixteenth century, they banned the quipu method of communicating – though it lived on in pockets of memory.

Five hundred years later, Cecilia still keeps this tradition alive. Like Sheila Hicks, she encourages us to look and touch, but also listen. Often, you'll hear a soundtrack of Quechua music when walking through Cecilia's quipu 'forests'.

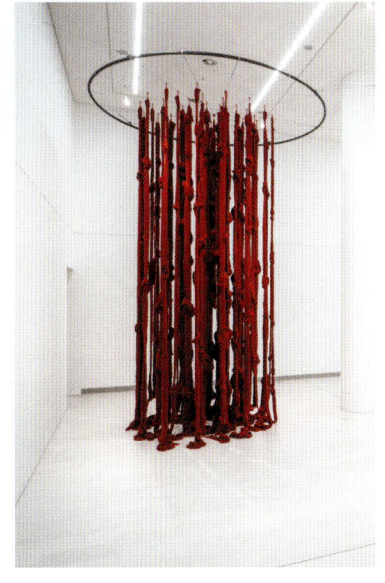

CECILIA VICUÑA, *QUIPU WOMB (THE STORY OF THE RED THREAD, ATHENS)*, 2017.

The artist **JUDITH SCOTT** born in 1943 in Ohio, USA, also used fibre to communicate. She was born deaf and with a condition called Down Syndrome. Judith had a twin sister called Joyce, born without disabilities. The two were very close.

But when they were just seven years old, Judith was sent to live in an institution for people with disabilities. Unlike today, these places treated their patients very unfairly, and Judith endured horrible conditions.

Joyce always wanted to find her sister and, thirty-five years later, they were finally reunited. Joyce took Judith home to live with her and her daughters in Oakland, California.

Near Judith's new home was an art centre called Creative Growth, which encouraged people with disabilities to take part in art workshops. For the first two years, Judith didn't touch anything. But, after she attended a fibre art workshop, she couldn't stop bundling together bits of thread and rope. She continued to do this for the rest of her life.

Judith never spoke with words, but she communicated using fibre. Art can be a way for us to interact and express ourselves, our thoughts and emotions, even if we don't quite know what they mean.

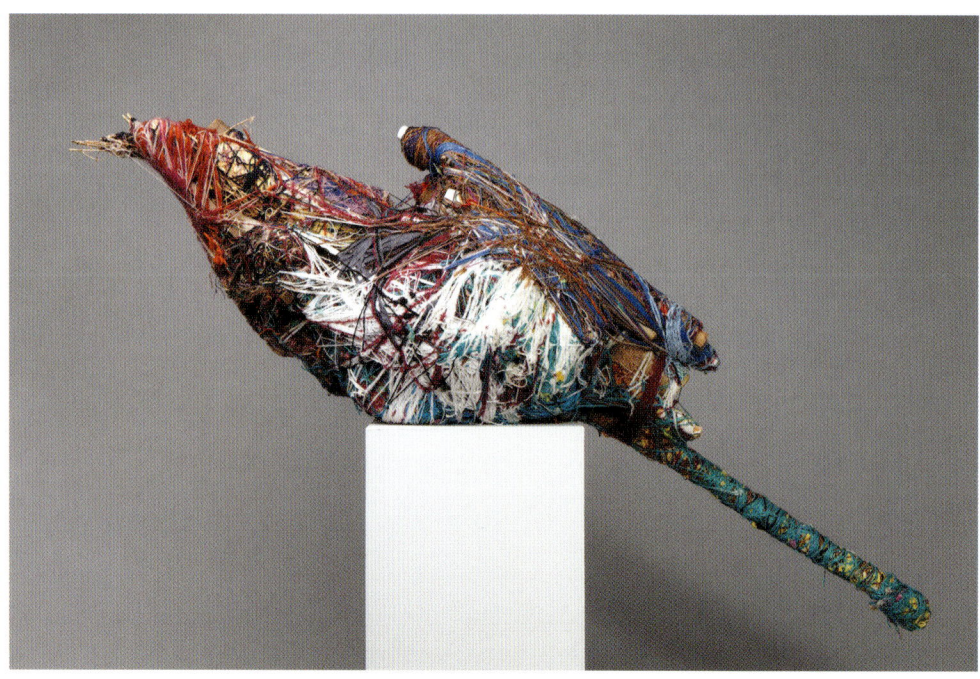

JUDITH SCOTT, *UNTITLED*, 1997.

Look closely at Judith's work. This one might look like a bird, but it's actually all sorts of objects bundled up in different coloured threads (to me, the tail could be the other end of a cricket bat!). With all these secret objects inside, it's as if only Judith knows the true meaning of her art.

You can create textile-based artworks out of anything – even old clothes, like jeans! That's what the **GEE'S BEND QUILTMAKERS** do. In their own words, they like to 'make something shine from something that's been thrown away'.

The Gee's Bend Quiltmakers are an all-female, Black American community based in Alabama, USA, comprised of more than four generations of women. They make their colourful and jazzy quilts for all different reasons – for art, but also for warmth and to keep the mosquitoes out.

LORETTA PETTWAY BENNETT, *WORK-CLOTHES STRIPS*, 2003.

For this jean-themed quilt, Loretta Pettway Bennett used her husband's and son's trousers!

ART TASK
Isn't it extraordinary all the different ways artists use textiles? Next time you outgrow a pair of jeans or a T-shirt, have a go at making something out of them, using the artists in this chapter as inspiration.

THE 1970S AND THE FEMINIST MOVEMENT

Throughout history, people have challenged injustice and tried to make the world a fairer place. The 1970s were no different – this was a decade of revolution.

It followed the Civil Rights Movement of the 1950s and 1960s, when Black communities across the United States pushed for fairer opportunities. And it came after the Stonewall Uprising of 1969, where people took to the streets to protest homophobia.

In the late 1960s and 1970s, feminists around the world campaigned for equal rights for women, across all areas of life and work – including art. Before this, women artists were barely taught about in schools, or seen on museum walls.

SO THE WOMEN OF THE 1970S DECIDED TO DO SOMETHING ABOUT IT.

In 1970, **LINDA NOCHLIN**, a trailblazing art historian who worked at Vassar College in upstate New York, began one of the first-ever university courses devoted to women artists. The following year, she wrote a famous essay, 'Why Have There Been No Great Women Artists?'. Now, just to be clear, Linda was certainly not saying that there are no talented women artists. Instead, she was asking why the world would not consider these women as some of the greats. The answer was because women were seen as inferior to men in society and in many areas of life. So they were rarely given the recognition or the opportunities they deserved.

Something had to be done. So Linda put on a groundbreaking exhibition with her friend and fellow art historian **ANN SUTHERLAND HARRIS**, featuring 400 years of art by women – including many of the artists you've learned about in this book!

American artist **JUDY CHICAGO**, born in 1939, was also fed up with not learning enough about brilliantly creative women. So, in 1974 she decided to construct a giant artwork, which she called *The Dinner Party*. She assembled a giant triangular table, each side measuring 14 metres long (about the length of a bus!), and set thirty-nine place names on the table that celebrated incredible women from history and mythology.

THIS SOUNDS LIKE MY DREAM DINNER PARTY!

Some of the guests included artists Georgia O'Keeffe and Artemisia Gentileschi, writer Virginia Woolf and abolitionist Sojourner Truth, who fought against slavery. Judy and a team of skilled craftspeople hand-embroidered place settings for all the women, sculpted ceramic plates, and added cups and cutlery.

ART TASK
If you were to design your own version of *The Dinner Party*, who would you choose to honour? Maybe your favourite singer? Or an artist from this book? Or someone in your family?

JUDY CHICAGO, DETAIL OF THE VIRGINIA WOOLF PLACE SETTING (LEFT), *THE DINNER PARTY*, 1974–9 (RIGHT).

Look closely at the middle of the table, and you'll see the names of 999 more women written on the shiny white porcelain!

With the feminist movement in full swing, artists also wanted to use their work to support other women.

In 1971, Faith Ringgold (see page 118) made striking posters with bold colours and letters, and the slogan: 'WOMAN FREEDOM NOW'.

'ANYONE CAN FLY, ALL YOU GOTTA DO IS TRY.'
– FAITH RINGGOLD

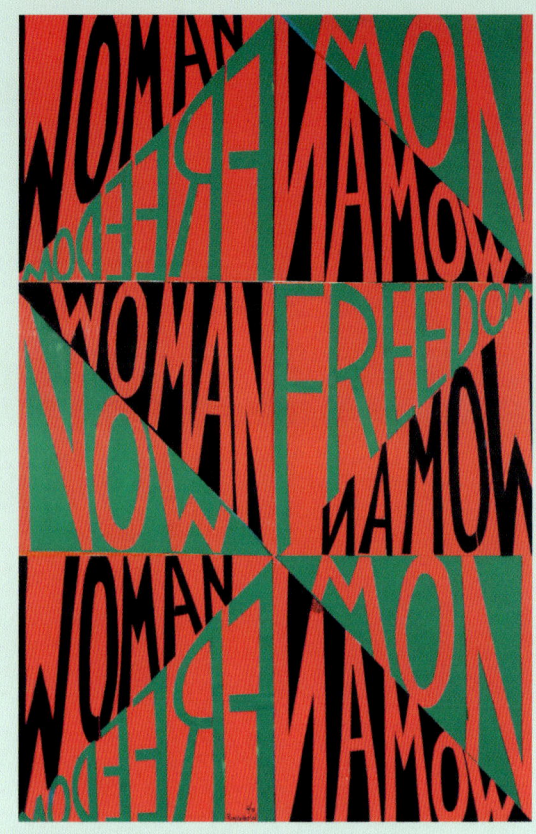

FAITH RINGGOLD, WOMAN FREEDOM NOW, 1971.

Faith also wanted to bring hope to female prisoners, and did this by making a giant painting called *For the Women's House*. Displayed at the Women's House of Detention, a prison in New York City, it was divided into eight triangles, which each featured pictures of women in different professional roles.

FAITH RINGGOLD, FOR THE WOMEN'S HOUSE, 1971.

What can you see? I can spot a bus driver, basketball players, doctors, teachers and more. Art can be a brilliant way of sharing messages of hope and positivity. Faith wanted to show the women prisoners that life can get better. If you can see something, then it starts to feel possible.

Then there was the American artist **ALICE NEEL**, who was born in 1900. She loved to paint people in her 'expressive' style. This means she focused more on capturing their personality, rather than what they simply looked like. Alice painted as many people as she could, in her community and beyond – fellow artists, writers, taxi drivers, cleaners, political figures, neighbours, her family and anonymous citizens.

> Here is Neel's painting of Linda Nochlin – the trailblazing writer from the beginning of this chapter. She is sitting with her wide-eyed daughter, Daisy, at Alice's apartment in New York City. Can you see how many colours there are on her face? That's Alice's way of capturing Linda's personality. I also like how Alice has put Daisy at the centre of this picture, even though Linda is the famous one. For me, it shows hope and belief in the next generation of women.

ALICE NEEL, *LINDA NOCHLIN AND DAISY*, 1973.

ALICE NEEL, *BENJAMIN*, 1976.

> This is Benjamin, the son of the caretaker who looked after Alice's apartment building. It sort of looks like he's sat for the painting because he's waiting around for his parents (I know the feeling!).

Alice's paintings include people of all ages and backgrounds. She wanted to show that everyone is worthy of being in the history of art. This was the aim of many women artists working in the 1970s. They used their art to represent and inspire hope among everyday people, and to uncover stories that were previously hidden from view.

ART CAN SHOW US A DIFFERENT PERSPECTIVE, AND INSPIRE A BETTER, FAIRER WORLD.

THE 1980S

By the 1980s, art was no longer just about painting or sculpture. Instead, artists began to reflect what was on city streets and in the media. Art could now also include billboards, advertisements and films.

While the 1970s had been a time of great progress for women artists, sadly it wasn't enough. In fact, it still isn't enough! Today London's National Gallery dedicates just 1 per cent of its collection to women artists even though women make up half the world population! Pretty imbalanced, don't you think?

In 1985, a group of women artists called the **GUERRILLA GIRLS** came together to protest this. They wanted to be anonymous, so they wore gorilla masks to hide their faces. They would get up in the middle of the night when everyone was asleep, go out into the streets of New York City and glue posters on walls of nearby museums.

Although they wore 'gorilla' masks, they called themselves Guerrilla Girls. Guerrilla is a word that refers to small, independent groups who fight against larger forces – like these women taking on the big museums!

These posters revealed some shocking facts. They deliberately used bold text to make them look like advertisements, so more people would take notice.

One poster asked: 'How Many Women Had One-Person Exhibitions at NYC (New York City) Museums Last Year?' The poster revealed that big important museums like the Guggenheim had 0, the Met had 0, the Modern (now MoMA) had 1, and the Whitney had 0.

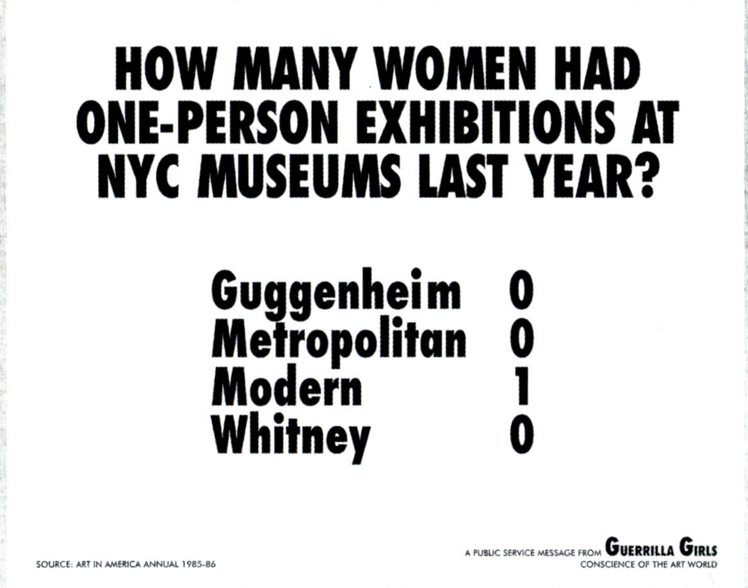

A ONE-PERSON SHOW
A one-person exhibition is an show by an individual artist, rather than a group of artists.

HOW MANY WOMEN HAD ONE-PERSON EXHIBITIONS AT NYC MUSEUMS LAST YEAR?

Guggenheim	0
Metropolitan	0
Modern	1
Whitney	0

SOURCE: ART IN AMERICA ANNUAL 1985-86 · A PUBLIC SERVICE MESSAGE FROM GUERRILLA GIRLS CONSCIENCE OF THE ART WORLD

GUERRILLA GIRLS, *HOW MANY WOMEN HAD ONE-PERSON EXHIBITIONS AT NYC MUSEUMS LAST YEAR?*, 1985.

They used humour in a lot of their work, which is a great way to grab people's attention. Here, in The Advantages Of Being A Woman Artist, 1988, they show us all the disadvantages, but sarcastically call them 'advantages'. These include 'Working without the pressure of success', because back then it was very rare for a woman artist to be successful.

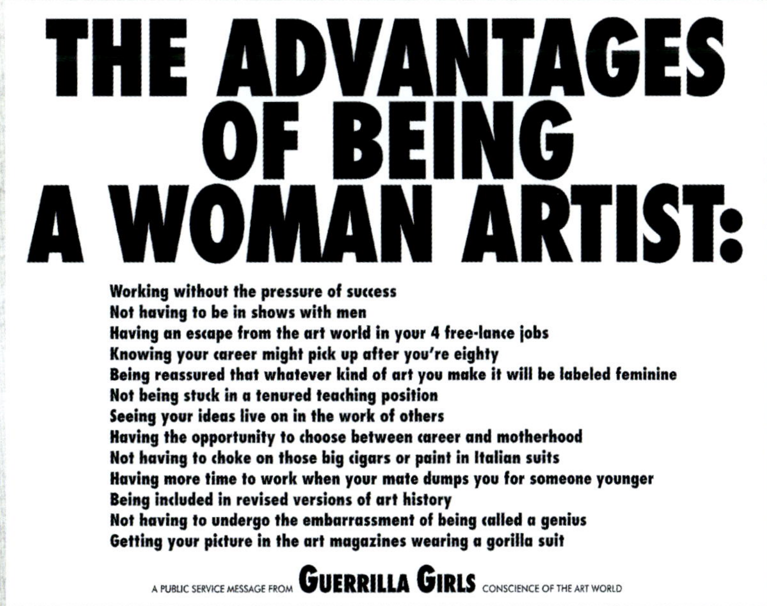

THE ADVANTAGES OF BEING A WOMAN ARTIST:

Working without the pressure of success
Not having to be in shows with men
Having an escape from the art world in your 4 free-lance jobs
Knowing your career might pick up after you're eighty
Being reassured that whatever kind of art you make it will be labeled feminine
Not being stuck in a tenured teaching position
Seeing your ideas live on in the work of others
Having the opportunity to choose between career and motherhood
Not having to choke on those big cigars or paint in Italian suits
Having more time to work when your mate dumps you for someone younger
Being included in revised versions of art history
Not having to undergo the embarrassment of being called a genius
Getting your picture in the art magazines wearing a gorilla suit

A PUBLIC SERVICE MESSAGE FROM **GUERRILLA GIRLS** CONSCIENCE OF THE ART WORLD

GUERRILLA GIRLS, *THE ADVANTAGES OF BEING A WOMAN ARTIST*, 1988.

I bought this in a museum shop and had it on my bedroom wall when I was growing up!

The Guerrilla Girls show us the creative ways in which we can protest against unfairness and injustice – and how to have fun while we're at it!

The 1980s were a booming time for films. But films back then were a little different to how they are now. Women were typically cast in 'supporting' roles, which usually involved working for a man, or simply being there for him to fall in love with. By contrast, men played heroes, leaders and bosses, and interesting characters with cool background stories.

Artists wanted to play around with what they were seeing on-screen. By this time, cameras were much cheaper, so more people were able to use them for their art. Women used photography to recreate (and poke fun at) the way male film directors were representing women.

CINDY SHERMAN, born in New Jersey in 1954, dressed up in different outfits and wore make-up and wigs and then photographed herself as the typical characters women were cast to play. This might be a housewife, secretary, or just someone who cared a lot about their appearance. At first, she created shots that looked just like 'film stills' (a frozen moment from a real film).

CINDY SHERMAN, *UNTITLED FILM STILL #10*, 1978.

She called these photographs her 'Untitled Film Stills, 1977–80'. Perhaps she chose 'Untitled' because she wanted to leave it up to the viewer to work out what was going on. What do you imagine is the scene or situation around the female character in the picture?

CINDY SHERMAN, *UNTITLED FILM STILL #56*, 1980.

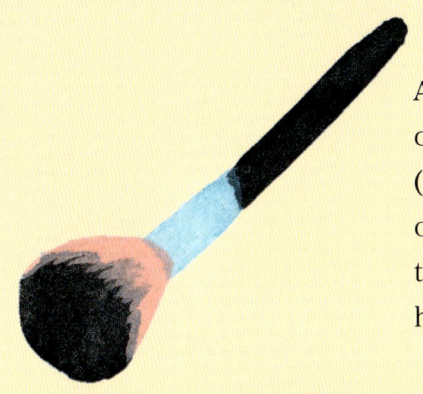

As the years went on, Cindy's dressing-up got more outrageous. Still working today, she wears prosthetics (plastic implants) to make her facial features look very over-the-top, or tons of make-up and fake tan. And I mean tons! This is to highlight how ridiculous beauty standards have become for women.

I think she wanted us to think twice about how women were expected to look and behave.

CINDY SHERMAN, *UNTITLED*, 2003

'I FEEL I'M ANONYMOUS IN MY WORK. WHEN I LOOK AT THE PICTURES, I NEVER SEE MYSELF; THEY AREN'T SELF-PORTRAITS. SOMETIMES I DISAPPEAR.'
– CINDY SHERMAN

135

Then there were those who used art as a way to encourage people to take better care of the environment. They were trailblazers in getting people to think about protecting green spaces – for their own health, and to preserve the land for future generations.

Have you ever seen pictures of Manhattan in New York City? It's one of the busiest and most polluted islands in the world. From every corner you'll see a skyscraper. So, over four months in 1982, **AGNES DENES** (born in 1931 in Hungary) planted, grew and harvested a two-acre farm of wheat at the tip of Manhattan. (It was the size of one and a half football pitches!)

She called the work *Wheatfield – A Confrontation* because it was about 'confronting' how people were mistreating the land's natural resources. Although it no longer exists, Denes' artwork is now considered one of the most important public art projects in art history.

Can you spot the Statue of Liberty?

AGNES DENES, WHEATFIELD – A CONFRONTATION: BATTERY PARK LANDFILL, DOWNTOWN MANHATTAN – WITH STATUE OF LIBERTY ACROSS THE HUDSON, 1892.

By showing them side by side, Agnes highlighted the difference between the naturally growing wheat and the man-made buildings. It is a good reminder that even though everyone leads very busy lives, we need to slow down and remember the importance of nature and the plants that feed us, such as wheat, from which we make bread and other staples.

AGNES DENES, *WHEATFIELD – A CONFRONTATION: BATTERY PARK LANDFILL, DOWNTOWN MANHATTAN – WITH NEW YORK FINANCIAL CENTER*, 1892.

137

I ALWAYS SAY ANYONE IS WORTHY OF BEING INCLUDED IN ART.

When you think of art, what comes to mind? Is it a sculpture or a photograph? Is it something that makes you laugh, cry or want to change the world for the better?

The American artist **LORRAINE O'GRADY**, born in Boston, USA, in 1934, asked these questions in her work *Art Is...* She also wanted to show everyone, whoever they were, that they could be 'art' too.

This was important to Lorraine. The project was a response to someone who had made a false and cruel claim that modern art 'doesn't have anything to do with Black people'. She wanted to prove them wrong.

LORRAINE O'GRADY, *ART IS . . . (TROUPE WITH MLLE BOURGEOISE NOIRE)*, 1983.

I love these pictures: from little girls hugging and smiling, to grown men and women dancing, ART IS... celebrates the joy of art, and how it truly is for everyone.

On a glitteringly sunny day in 1983, she rented a giant float (a platform attached to a car or lorry) with a gold frame mounted on its front, and took her camera to Harlem's African-American Day Parade, which celebrates Black culture and heritage. She asked fifteen performers to dress up in white clothes and instructed them to hold up gold frames to people's faces in the crowds. This was to demonstrate that they belonged inside the frame, too.

LORRAINE O'GRADY, *ART IS . . . (DANCER IN GRASS SKIRT)*, 1983.

LORRAINE O'GRADY, *ART IS . . . (GIRLFRIENDS TIMES TWO)*, 1983.

ART TASK
What would your version of 'Art Is...' be? Who would you put inside the frame?

BRITAIN IN THE 1990S

In 1990s Britain, change was in the air. There was a new government: the younger, forward-thinking Labour Party replaced the more traditional Conservative Party, who had been in power for eighteen years. Bands like the Spice Girls formed, who were famous for promoting 'Girl Power'. Cities like London were developing and expanding at rapid pace. There was a new feeling of hope and optimism in the air.

Art, too, entered a whole new era, driven by young, ambitious, rule-breaking artists. They made work that was bold, loud and relatable, so everyone could connect with it, no matter their background. This was a refreshing change, as art had previously felt like something reserved for the wealthiest people in society.

Lots of these artists hadn't grown up with traditional art on the walls of their homes. Most of them were from working-class backgrounds, which meant their parents often worked in shops and factories and didn't earn a lot of money. As artists, they had to forge their own way.

They took a DIY (do-it-yourself) approach. Never waiting around for someone else's approval, or to be given a space in a gallery, they found abandoned warehouses on the edge of London, gave them a lick of paint, and hung up their art.

Some, like the English artists **SARAH LUCAS** and **TRACEY EMIN**, also opened shops to sell their art. Sarah and Tracey called theirs 'The Shop'. It was on a street in East London, and it had a fish pond!

Days before it opened in January 1993, they bought materials from the nearby Brick Lane market and made as much stuff as they could. When they opened, they sold their handmade badges and T-shirts with funny handwritten phrases like 'So boring' and 'She's Kebab'. This is them:

TRACEY EMIN, who is now Dame Tracey Emin, has opened her own art school in her home town of Margate. It's dedicated to educating future generations of artists.

The pair also changed the idea of what sculpture could look like. For example, Tracey installed her real-life bed in the middle of the Tate gallery (she called it *My Bed*). It was unmade, with her belongings scattered about.

You might be thinking: *How is this art?* Well, Tracey was essentially making a self-portrait through her belongings. Self-portraits don't always have to be exact likenesses of us; they can be of our stuff, too (like our bedsheets and pillows!). It's just another way of telling people about our experiences.

TRACEY EMIN, *MY BED*, 1998.

ART TASK
If you were to make a self-portrait from your belongings, which items would you choose, and what might they say about you?

These artists were full of new ideas and were often inspired by items found in their homes and everyday lives. Growing up in Essex, **RACHEL WHITEREAD**, born in 1963, had always been fascinated by cardboard boxes – particularly the ones that contain bits and bobs, like Christmas lights or old photographs.

ALTHOUGH THEY SEEM ORDINARY, THEY HOLD IMPORTANT MEMORIES.

In 1993, Rachel cast an entire terraced house! She poured concrete into the house and, once it had hardened, removed the walls of the house to show the solid air inside. *This took a whole month.* The old house was going to be demolished anyway as part of the redevelopment of London, so this was her way of preserving the memories of the people who had once lived inside it.

RACHEL WHITEREAD, *HOUSE*, 1993.

This is the result. It looks a little bit ghostly, don't you think? The opposite of a warm, cosy house.

But people weren't happy about this, and it even ended up being debated by politicians in Parliament, who argued over whether it should be taken down! It caused a huge scandal, as people didn't consider it 'art' and were shocked that public money was spent on it. It was demolished eleven weeks later.

In 1991, **CORNELIA PARKER**, born in Cheshire, England in 1956, created an artwork called *Cold Dark Matter: An Exploded View*, which involved blowing up a garden shed and suspending the remains from the ceiling. The blown-up items included old bikes, toys, drinks cans, wood (from the shed itself) and hair curlers.

> This method is not one to try at home. Parker even had help from soldiers in the British Army!

She hung all the items on metal wires and added a light bulb in the centre. This created strange, eerie shadows on the walls and floor. And, because the objects had been shattered into a million pieces, viewers were left asking questions about what they had once been.

CORNELIA PARKER, *COLD DARK MATTER: AN EXPLODED VIEW*, 1991.

> Look closely at this work. What can you see? Although it feels like we should hear a loud BANG!, the work is very quiet - like an explosion frozen in space and time...

Unlike a lot of artists we've looked at so far in this book, those in 1990s Britain worked 'in the real world' as opposed to sitting in a studio. It opened up people's eyes to the idea that there are many places to make art and to see it too. By being out and about, engaging with real people and places, they helped make art feel more relevant to people of all different backgrounds.

The photographer **GILLIAN WEARING**, born in Birmingham, England in 1963, worked directly with the public when it came to making her art. In the early 1990s, she wanted to know how people were feeling. So, she took her camera to the streets, with blank pieces of paper and a pen. Then she asked passers-by to write down their emotions, thoughts or feelings and to hold it up so she could photograph it.

Here are some of the results:

GILLIAN WEARING, Signs that say what you want them to say and not Signs that say what someone else wants you to say BEST FRIENDS FOR LIFE! LONG LIVE THE TWO OF US., 1992 (LEFT) AND I'M DESPERATE, 1992 (RIGHT)

What do you think of the answers? Do any of them surprise you? How does the man in the suit holding up the sign saying 'I'm desperate' make you feel? Sad or worried? Or the two smiling girls who wrote 'Best friends for life! Long live the two of us'. Does it remind you of a best friend you have?

ART TASK
What would you write? Or why don't you try this out on friends or family? It might reveal more about them than you expect.

The artists of the 1990s were all about changing traditions. They were fearless in their approach, unafraid to be bold and to ask questions. As a result, London became one of the creative centres of the world. This, as we will find out later in the book (page 152), spawned new galleries, the likes of which had seemed unimaginable before . . .

FIRST NATIONS ART IN AUSTRALIA

Australia is the biggest island in the world. But it is also a continent, made up of many different communities. Lots of these communities are First Nations cultural groups, who speak over 300 languages.

Indigenous people live all around Australia and are called 'First Nations' because their communities inhabited Australia before the British invaded the country in 1788.

'Country' is the term used by First Nations Australian people to describe the land, waterways, sea and sky. It's through art that First Nations people show what it feels like to live in and care for Country, capturing the blaring heat, starry skies, the gusts of wind, rain and spirit.

On first glance, these paintings might appear abstract. But once you look carefully, you'll start to understand that each mark or brushstroke corresponds to something in nature.

For example, look at this dazzling work by **ALMA NUNGARRAYI GRANITES**, a Warlpiri woman who lived in Yuendumu, Northern Territory, Central Desert region of Australia. Astronomy and the cosmic world are important to First Nations people. They are way of measuring the seasons, understanding which month of the year it is and navigating your way in the night (like a compass).

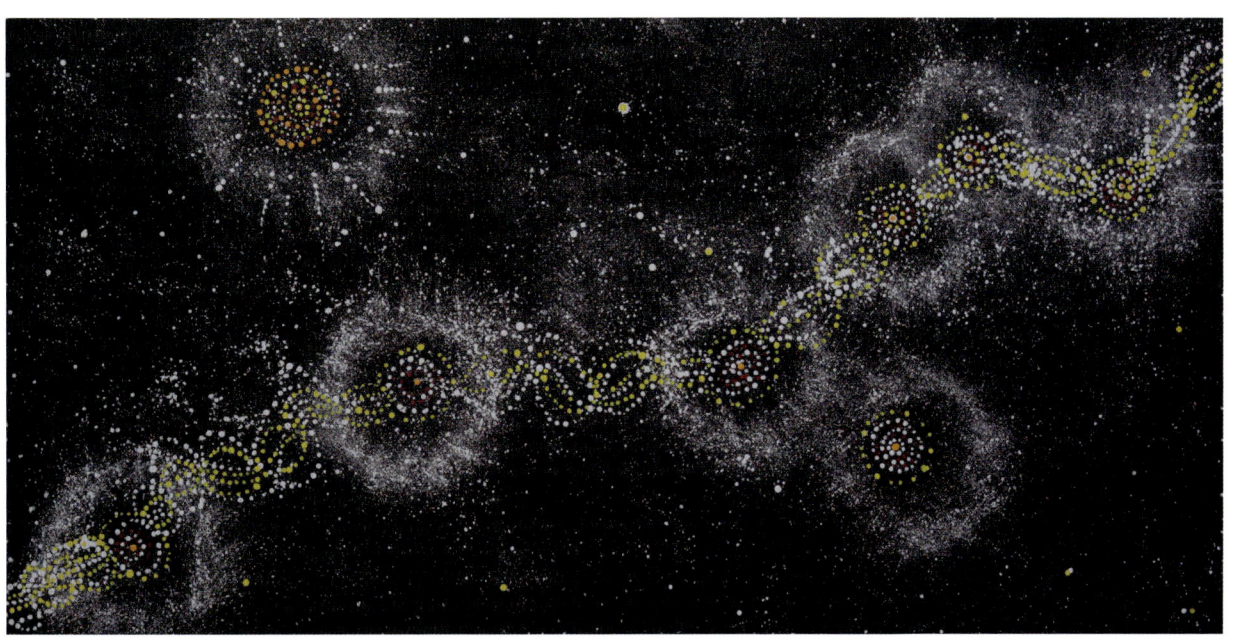

ALMA NUNGARRAYI GRANITES, *NAPALJARRI-WARNU JUKURRPA* (STAR OR SEVEN SISTERS DREAMING, 2011.

What at first appears to be bursts of white rings and yellow snake-like lines actually demonstrate the amazing stars found in this area of the desert. Where I live, in London, you can hardly see the stars because of light pollution. But in the remote Australian town where Alma is from, stars fill the sky like a shimmering blanket.

147

Instead of painting on an easel, many First Nations artists work by sitting together on the floor with their canvases on the ground in front of them. Some paintings are made communally – so in groups, with sisters, aunts, cousins or daughters. Painting with Elders and listening to their stories while creating beautiful paintings together is part of First Nations culture. Passing on stories orally (by speaking) is a way of keeping Indigenous knowledge alive.

This luminous painting, *Seven Sisters*, was made in 2018 by five sisters of the Ken family: **FREDA BRADY**, **TJUNGKARA KEN**, **SANDRA KEN**, **MARINGKA TUNKIN** and **YARITJI YOUNG**. They are from the First Nations people known as the Pitjantjatjara, who live in a community called Amata.

TJUNGKARA KEN, SANDRA KEN, YARITJI YOUNG, FREDA BRADY, MARINGKA TUNKIN, PITJANTJATJARA PEOPLE, *SEVEN SISTERS*, 2018.

The title *Seven Sisters* refers to a First Nations creation story that extends across Australia, about the star constellations of Pleiades and Orion. It follows seven sisters, who come together when one is chased by a bad man. It's about the importance of families protecting each other. Speaking about the work, the Ken sisters have said: 'When we work together as a family we are learning from each other and teaching each other.'

KATHLEEN NGAL, born in 1934, and her sisters are famous for being the most accomplished painters in their region of Utopia, Northern Territory, which is just north of Australia's central point.

> In this painting, Kathleen uses thousands of dots of colour to represent rain. But it's also a map of her region, showing where prized fruits can be found.

KATHLEEN NGAL, *UNTITLED*, 2010.

ART TASK
If you were to draw the feeling of the landscape (or skyscape) where you live, what would you create?

One of Australia's most significant artists was the great **EMILY KAM KNGWARRAY**. She made over 3,000 paintings in her lifetime, but she only began painting when she was in her seventies! That's the equivalent of creating one painting per day. And they're not small: many measure up to eight metres wide (the length of a volleyball court).

EMILY KAM KNGWARRAY, *YAM AWELY*, 1995.

Emily was also from Utopia. I find her paintings mesmerizing – explosions of colour made out of lines running in different directions. Emily saw her home landscape as alive and that's what her paintings help us to understand, too. It's like she's capturing every animal as it scurries under a rock, or plays in a river stream. And all of this life sits under the burning heat of an Australian summer.

This painting is called **YAM AWELY**. 'Yam' is a word for the flowering yam, which Emily identified with. 'Awely' is a ceremony where one is in touch with their spiritual self. It translates to 'my dreamings'. You can really tell Emily loved her Country.

First Nations artists also paint on different surfaces, such as pieces of bark, or, in the case of Kitty Kantilla, wooden figures. This is Purrukuparli and Wai-ai.

KITTY KANTILLA, *WAI-AI* (LEFT) AND *PURRUKUPARLI* (RIGHT), 1995.

A NEW ART FOR THE MILLENNIUM

As we near the end of the book – and edge closer to the present day – it's difficult to know which works will define this age. Especially because some of those works are probably being made right now! It's easier to look back in art history and see how artworks defined that era. So for this chapter, I've focused on art that I believe had the biggest impact at the turn of the millennium.

ONE THING'S FOR SURE: THE SCALE OF ART GALLERIES HAS CHANGED DRAMATICALLY. In the year 2000, I was six. I know what you're thinking: *She's so old*. But I still remember it like it was yesterday. I grew up in London, where at the stroke of a new century and millennium, a new gallery opened: Tate Modern.

No one had ever seen anything like it. Sat on the bank of the River Thames, it was an old power station, with a giant turbine hall (a room that once contained electricity generators). The space, now called the Turbine Hall, measures a staggering 35 metres high (the same height as twelve classrooms stacked on top of each other) and 152 metres long (three times the length of an Olympic swimming pool). Pretty big, right?

> This is what the Turbine Hall looked like before.

> But after a bit of refurbishment, it became a gallery.

DORIS SALCEDO, *SHIBBOLETH II*, 2007.

Dedicated to showing contemporary art (the name given to art made in the present day), the gallery gave artists a whole new dimension to work with. Artwork could now expand out in any direction: it could be huge, small, or in millions of different pieces – fixed to the ceiling or placed on the floor.

In my lifetime I've seen a giant screen in the shape of a sun that lit up the whole room; electric mushroom-shaped flying robots (called 'aerobes'); 100 million artificial sunflower seeds scattered out on the floor – and much more!

RACHEL WHITEREAD, *EMBANKMENT*, 2005.

> One time, Rachel Whiteread (see page 143) filled the gallery with tens of thousands of empty white boxes! It felt like snowy mountains had descended on the museum. I couldn't decide whether they felt heavy, or full of air.

ART TASK
Imagine the Tate Modern asked you to fill this room. Keep in mind that the Turbine Hall is free to access, and anyone can come in and see your show. Millions of people visit every year. What would you like to fill it with?

153

Throughout my childhood, the Tate Modern was my favourite place to go. I'd visit on a Saturday afternoon or during school holidays with my friends. There are lots of rooms to explore, with exhibitions of all kinds. You have to pay for some of them, but most of it is free!

The first artist invited to show their work in the new Turbine Hall was **LOUISE BOURGEOIS**, born in Paris in 1911. One of her artworks was a colossal sculpture of a spider, 9 metres high! Personally, I'm scared of spiders, but Louise makes me see a different side to them. She called her spider *Maman* (which means 'mummy/mama' in French), as she views it as a protector and repairer. As she said:

'IF YOU BASH INTO THE WEB OF A SPIDER, SHE DOESN'T GET MAD. SHE WEAVES AND REPAIRS IT.'

LOUISE BOURGEOIS, *MAMAN*, 1999.

For another installation, an artist called **DORIS SALCEDO**, born in 1958, made us look a little harder.

Go back to the previous page and look at the photo of the refurbished gallery. What can you see?

Doris drilled a giant crack in the floor! Why do you think she did this? To me, she's saying that we must always look around us and take notice, otherwise we might miss something that's right in front of us.

Doris was born in Colombia, the same year that a civil war in her country finally came to an end. Known as La Violencia, which translates to 'The Violence', during the ten years of war many people lost their lives, more were injured, and even more had to leave their homes. Members of her own family disappeared – and this inspired her to make work from the point of view of innocent people.

This artwork in the Turbine Hall split the massive gallery in two. When I saw it, it got me thinking about the country borders that divide the world and put people at war with each other. Doris's crack permanently scarred the gallery's floor. If you visit Tate Modern and look closely today, you can still see it. For me, this is a reminder to never forget what innocent people have gone through in history.

When you think of a monument, what comes to mind? Maybe a sculpture of a president or a queen, the Statue of Liberty, or Pisa's famous leaning tower?

MONUMENTS OFTEN TELL A STORY FROM HISTORY, BUT THESE AREN'T ALWAYS THE HAPPIEST STORIES.

In 2019, an American artist called **KARA WALKER**, born in California, USA, in 1969, was driving past Buckingham Palace and noticed the Victoria Memorial that sits outside. This is a monument that honours Queen Victoria and the British Empire.

The British Empire is the term used to describe all the countries that Britain conquered and ruled over (more than fifty in total). It began in the late 1500s and was the most powerful empire in the world for nearly 400 years.

The Empire brought the country lots of wealth and power. But for many of the people ruled by Britain, the reality was a different story entirely. In particular, the British had a huge part to play in the cruel and violent transatlantic slave trade, which as we learned about on page 77, involved taking millions of African people from their homes and families, and forcing them to work in terrible conditions across Europe and the United States.

At Tate Modern, Kara wanted to create a new monument. Instead of celebrating the Empire, she wanted to present the point of view of the countries that Britain conquered. She made a fountain in the style of the Victoria Memorial but filled it with symbols and figures that drew attention to the parts of this history that are often overlooked.

KARA WALKER, *FONS AMERICANUS*, 2019.

> Kara showed the passage of the enslaved as they were shipped across the seas. The sculptures on the monument show the violent ways they were treated, and the racist beliefs that were promoted at this time.

Kara is just one of a number of artists challenging the world's monuments today. While they might look beautiful, it's important to understand what they are representing. Unfortunately, much of the time, they are cheering for a shameful history.

Fortunately, these monuments are being questioned more than ever. Art like Kara's has been such an important tool for starting these conversations and getting us to look at history from a different perspective.

ART IN PUBLIC SPACES HELPS US ALL TAKE PART IN THESE DISCUSSIONS AND SEE HOW, TOGETHER, WE CAN MAKE THE WORLD A BETTER, KINDER AND MORE EQUAL PLACE.

ART FOR THE NEW WORLD

What do you think the twenty-first century 'looks' like? If I asked you to draw, paint or sculpt it, what would you come up with?

The first thing that comes to my mind is screens – large ones, small ones, still ones, moving ones. From phones that fit in our pockets to the billboards that blare advertisements.

Through screens, we can connect with anyone in the world and access an infinite amount of information at a moment's notice. This has only really been possible in this century. So how can we represent this in art?

Let me introduce you to **SARAH SZE**, who was born in Boston, USA in 1969. In her art, she creates structures filled with screens of different sizes. Whenever I see her work in real life, it feels like stepping inside a dizzying laboratory.

> Sarah's works have been described as an 'exploded iPhone', and it really is like all the different pictures and frames that we see on a phone are suspended in space. Her work shows me just how much information we are consuming by the second!

SARAH SZE, *METRONOME*, 2023.

Another artist, **JULIE MEHRETU**, who was born in Ethiopia in 1970 and moved to the USA as a child, captures the speed of the twenty-first century through paint. Remember those artists working a hundred years ago, called the Futurists (page 65), who wanted to capture the speed of a boat racing through water in a painting? Julie takes things one step further.

From far away, her paintings look like the chaos of the whole world erupting. It reminds me of images of Earth from space. It might appear like a ball of cloud, sea and land, but when we're on it, it looks and feels completely different – made up of billions of individual lives, identities, places and cultures.

JULIE MEHRETU, *EMPIRICAL CONSTRUCTION, ISTANBUL*, 2003.

> Because when you take a closer look at this work, you can see tiny maps and architectural drawings of real places, such as the the Hagia Sophia in Istanbul (a church that was converted to a mosque, then to a museum). Or colours symbolic of flags, cultures or nations – things that make the world unique.

PORTRAITURE

'PORTRAITS ARE VERY POWERFUL. THEY HAVE A GREAT REPRESENTATION AND DOMINANCE IN THE WORLD . . .'
– MICKALENE THOMAS

Right at the beginning of the book, we looked at portraits. So, given this chapter is about the modern world, why are portraits still relevant today?

In history, the same type of people were painted over and over again. Normally these people were wealthy or royal, such as this opulent family portrait by the seventeenth-century Italian painter **LAVINIA FONTANA**. It's of the Italian noblewoman Bianca degli Utili Maselli and six of her children (and their little dog!) all dressed in fancy, matching outfits.

LAVINIA FONTANA, *BIANCA DEGLI UTILI MASELLI WITH SIX OF HER CHILDREN*, c. 1604–5.

By only showing certain communities, many people remained invisible. It seems that artists today are making up for lost time, and painting people who have also always deserved to be on museum walls, no matter their background or status. As Mickalene says, portraits are powerful. If we can see ourselves on museum walls, then we might be inspired to become artists ourselves.

When the American artist **MICKALENE THOMAS** (born in 1971 in New Jersey, USA) was studying law at university, she wasn't sure if she could be an artist. But then she visited an exhibition by one of her heroes, artist **CARRIE MAE WEEMS** (born in 1953, in Portland, USA). It was Carrie's series of photographs, called the 'Kitchen Table Series', that caught Mickalene's attention.

CARRIE MAE WEEMS, *UNTITLED (WOMAN AND DAUGHTER WITH MAKEUP) FROM KITCHEN TABLE SERIES*, 1990.

They picture the everyday life of a Black woman around her kitchen table, from having dinner with family to - my favourite - putting on make-up with her daughter.

These photographs gave Mickalene the courage to become an artist. Why? Because she saw a life just like hers reflected in art, and thought: *I can tell my story, too.* Mickalene creates dazzling pictures, crafted with paint and glittering crystals, which make the people in her paintings 'shine'.

MICKALENE THOMAS, *LE DEJEUNER SUR L'HERBE: LES TROIS FEMMES NOIRES*, 2010.

She fills her canvases with proud, bold and glamorous Black women, who might be friends, lovers or family.

161

CHANTAL JOFFE (born in 1969) lives in London and paints people 'from life'. This means that people come to her studio and chat with her over a cup of tea as she paints them (including me!).

Chantal doesn't mind that the people in her paintings don't look realistic. She cares more about capturing how she and her subject felt on that particular day. But she does say that having someone in front of her can be a bit nerve-wracking.

CHANTAL JOFFE, *KATY IN A YELLOW SUIT*, 2023.

This is a painting of me. When she painted it, I didn't know how it was going to turn out. But I guess this was how Chantal saw me that day. I think I look quite deep in thought. What do you think?

Chantal likes to paint the same person lots of times. Her daughter, Es, is grown up now, but she was painted throughout her life by her mother, who captured her at different ages.

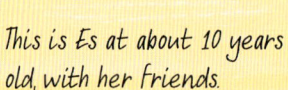

This is Es at about 10 years old, with her friends.

And getting ready for prom.

Here is Chantal with Es as a toddler. The two of them are clearly wrapped up in love, their bodies becoming one.

CHANTAL JOFFE, *SELF-PORTRAIT WITH ESME*, 2009 (LEFT). *POPPY, ESME, OLEANNA, GRACIE AND KATE*, 2014 (CENTRE). *PROM*, 2022 (RIGHT).

ART TASK

Why don't you draw someone close to you 'from life'? See how they might appear in different portraits made on different days. The drawing might change depending on how you felt that day. Painting from life is exciting – a bit like writing a diary. You might never feel the same again as you did on that day.

ZANELE MUHOLI, born in South Africa in 1972, uses photography to take self-portraits. They dress up with crowns and chunky jewellery, which make them appear like royalty.

But look closer, and you'll notice they're actually using items that can be easily found in the home – like clothes pegs!

Muholi is a LGBTQIA+ activist, who also uses a camera to tell positive stories of their LGBTQIA+ community. Sadly, in South Africa, where Zanele is from, these communities have often been treated unfairly, so taking dignified pictures of them is a way to pay them respect.

By playing on a royal 'look', they show that everyone is worthy of being in a portrait, no matter the price of the objects they're adorned with.

ZANELE MUHOLI, *BESTER I, MAYOTTE*, 2015.

Portraits don't have to be of specific people. They can be of anyone. In 2023, the National Portrait Gallery in London reopened to spectacular acclaim. The museum had drastically increased the amount of art *by* women and *of* women. They even dedicated an entire gallery to self-portraits by women! I loved it. It was incredible to see these artists I admired revealing how they saw themselves.

HARRY WELLER, *DETAIL OF A PANEL OF THE DOORS, WITH TRACEY EMIN*, 2023.

TRACEY EMIN, who we met on page 141, was invited to create portraits for the museum's doors. But rather than depicting specific people, she created portraits of 'moods'. This meant she could, in her words, represent 'every woman, every age and every culture throughout time'. So, no matter who walked into the gallery, they might feel seen and represented.

CONCLUSION

There are so many more trailblazing artists who I wish I could have included in this book. We've covered just a fraction of the great art made by women over the last 500 years. All over the world, you can find more artworks and artists to discover and celebrate.

I hope this book has shown you that there's no right or wrong way to enjoy art. What we have to do, as viewers, is to give artwork time, and ask questions. How does it make me feel? What kind of person made this, and why? Does it remind me of anything? Remember, the power of art is in experiencing it, interpreting it and speaking to others about it. Don't be afraid to say what you think, and ask other people what they think, too. Art is there to be discussed.

Just because something might not resonate with you, or someone else, now, doesn't mean that it won't in the future. Or it might be that when you hear someone else's interpretation of a piece of art it can take on a whole new meaning for you.

Some art has been around a lot longer than us. Although the art hasn't changed, the world around it has – drastically. Each generation and each individual brings with them their own thoughts about art.

Art can be an incredible thing to help us understand how people in the past lived their lives. If these artists hadn't made their art, then we wouldn't know what it felt like to live in Italy 400 years ago, or in Japan during the Second World War. Isn't it amazing to be able to learn about the past in this way?

Although nobody knows what kinds of artwork will define the world we're living in right now, it's interesting to think about how many artists today are looking back to the past, reclaiming traditions and working in similar materials and styles as artists 500 years ago.

Take, for instance, **FLORA YUKHNOVICH**, who was born in Norwich, England, in 1990. She makes giant paintings with a twist.

FLORA YUKHNOVICH, *SHE IS BEAUTY AND SHE IS GRACE*, 2022.

Aren't her paintings incredible? Flora uses oil paint and likes to reference ancient stories, just like those artists who worked in the Renaissance and Baroque periods. Sometimes she names her paintings after pop songs so we think about the relationship between history and world today.

I have loved sharing some of my favourite artists with you in this book. But really, the best way to experience art is in person. Why not head to a museum or gallery to see an artwork for yourself? There are so many all over the world built for everyone to enjoy. That's their purpose – for people to come and visit them. Don't be put off if a museum is in a rather grand, old building. Museums probably look like that because they've been welcoming people for hundreds of years!

And when you get there, why not write or draw what you see? You could even start your very own art diary. I've left a few blank pages at the end of this book for you to write about the art and artists you discover.

SO NOW YOU CAN BEGIN TO MAKE YOUR VERY OWN STORY OF ART!

ARTWORK CREDITS

Photographs are kindly provided by the artists and galleries listed, unless otherwise stated.

p.21. Sofonisba Anguissola, *The Game of Chess*, 1555. National Museum, Poznań, Poland. Photo: Artefact/Alamy.

p.22. Sofonisba Anguissola, *Bernardino Campi Painting Sofonisba Anguissola*, c.1559. Pinacoteca Nazionale, Siena. Photo: Artefact/Alamy.

p.24 (left). Properzia de' Rossi, *Joseph and Potiphar's Wife, 1525–6. Museo di San Petronio, Bologna.* Photo: Picture Art Collection/Alamy.

p.24 (right). Properzia de' Rossi, *Grassi Family Crest*, 1510–30. Museo Civico Medievale, Bologna.

p.25 (top left and right). Clara Peeters, *Still Life with a Vase of Flowers, Goblets and Shells*, 1612. Staatliche Kunsthalle, Karlsruhe. Photo: akg-images/Erich Lessing.

p.25 (bottom). Giovanna Garzoni, *Dog with a Biscuit and a Chinese Cup*, 1640s. Galleria Palatina di Palazzo Pitti, Florence. Photo: Nicolò Orsi Battaglini/Bridgeman Images.

p.28. Artemisia Gentileschi, *Judith and her Maidservant with the Head of Holofernes*, c.1623–5. Detroit Institute of Arts, Gift of Mr. Leslie H. Green, 52.253.

p.29. Artemisia Gentileschi, *Self-portrait as Saint Catherine of Alexandria*, c.1615–7. National Gallery, London. Photo: Bridgeman Images.

p.30. Judith Leyster, *Self-portrait*, c.1630. National Gallery of Art, Washington, D.C. Gift of Mr. and Mrs. Robert Woods Bliss, 1949.6.1.

p.31 (top). Judith Leyster, *The Serenade*, 1629. Rijksmuseum, Amsterdam.

p.31 (bottom). Rachel Ruysch, *Still Life with Flowers on a Marble Tabletop*, 1716. Rijksmuseum, Amsterdam.

p.32 (left to right). Mary Delany, Geranium Zonale, *Sea Daffodil and Passiflora Quadrangularis*, 1778. British Museum, London. © Trustees of the British Museum.

p.33. Maria Sibylla Merian, *Pomegranate and Menelaus Blue Morpho Butterfly*, 1702–3. Illustration from Metamorphosis insectorum Surinamensium, 1719.

p.35. Angelica Kauffman, *Design*, 1778–80. Royal Academy of Arts, London. Photo: John Hammond.

p.36. Johann Joseph Zoffany, *The Academicians of the Royal Academy*, 1771–72. Royal Collection Trust. Photo: © His Majesty King Charles III, 2026/Bridgeman Images.

p.37. Angelica Kauffmann, *Self-portrait as singer, holding a sheet of music*, 1753. Tiroler Landesmuseum Ferdinandeum, Innsbruck.

p.38. Emma Civey Stahl, *Woman's Rights Quilt*, c.1875. Metropolitan Museum of Art, New York. Funds from various donors, 2011.

p.39. Harriet Powers, *Pictorial Quilt*, 1895–8. Museum of Fine Arts, Boston. Bequest of Maxim Karolik. Photo: © 2026 MFA Boston. All rights reserved/Bridgeman Images.

p.42. Emily Mary Osborn, *Nameless and Friendless*, 1857. Private collection. Photo: Bridgeman Images.

p.43. Florence Claxton, *Women's Work: A Medley*, 1861. Manchester City Art Gallery, Manchester. Photo: Bridgeman Images.

p.44. Illustration of the Camera Obscura principle, eighteenth century. Photo: Science Photo Library.

p.45 (top). Julia Margaret Cameron's camera at Dimbola Lodge, Isle of Wight. Photo: Julia Margaret Cameron Trust.

p.45 (bottom left). Julia Margaret Cameron, *The Rosebud Garden of Girls*, 1868. J Paul Getty Museum, Malibu.

p.45 (bottom right). Julia Margaret Cameron, *Pomona*, 1872. Metropolitan Museum of Art, New York. David Hunter McAlpin Fund, 1963.

p.46 (top). Joanna Boyce Wells, *Study of Fanny Eaton*, 1861. Yale Center for British Art, New Haven. Paul Mellon Fund.

p.46 (bottom). Evelyn de Morgan, *Night and Sleep*, 1878. De Morgan Collection, courtesy of the De Morgan Foundation. Photo: Bridgeman Images.

p.47 (left). Anna Atkins, *Aspidium angulare*, from *Cyanotypes of British and Foreign Ferns*, 1853. J Paul Getty Museum of Art, Malibu.

p.47 (right). Anna Atkins, *Spiraea aruncus (Tyrol)*, from *Cyanotypes of British and Foreign Ferns* 1851–4. Metropolitan Museum of Art, New York. Purchase, Alfred Stieglitz Society Gifts, 2004.

p.50. Berthe Morisot, *The Artist's Sister at a Window*, 1869. National Gallery of Art, Washington, D.C. Ailsa Mellon Bruce Collection.

p.51. Berthe Morisot, *In the Garden at Maurecourt*, 1884. Toledo Museum of Art, Ohio. Purchased with funds from the Libbey Endowment. Gift of Edward Drummond Libbey.

p.52 (top left). Mary Cassatt, *Little Girl in a Blue Armchair*, 1878. National Gallery of Art, Washington, D.C. Collection of Mr. and Mrs. Paul Mellon.

p.52 (top right). Mary Cassatt, *Mother and Child (A Goodnight Hug)*, 1880. Private Collection. Photo: Christie's/Bridgeman Images.

p.52 (bottom). Mary Cassatt, *Young Girl Reading*, c.1894. Hirshhorn Museum & Sculpture Garden, Washington, D.C.

p.53. Marie Bashkirtseff, *Self-Portrait with a Palette*, 1883. Musée des Beaux-Arts Jules-Chéret, Nice. Photo: Picture Art Collection/Alamy.

p.55. Suzanne Valadon, *The Blue Room*, 1923. Musée National d'Art Moderne, Paris. Photo: Painters/Alamy.

p.56. Suzanne Valadon, *Raminou and Pitcher with Carnations*, 1932. Private Collection. Photo: Christie's/Bridgeman Images.

p.57 (top). Claude Cahun, *Self-Portrait Reflected in a Mirror,* 1927 Courtesy of Jersey Heritage Collections.

p.57 (bottom). Claude Cahun and Marcel Moore, Untitled (*Claude Cahun in Le Mystère d'Adam*), 1929. Gelatin silver print, 4 × 3 in. (10.16 × 7.62 cm). San Francisco Museum of Modern Art. Fractional and promised gift of Carla Emil and Rich Silverstein. Photo: Katherine Du Tiel/courtesy SFMOMA.

p.58. Amrita Sher-Gil, *Three Girls*, 1935. National Gallery of Modern Art, New Delhi.

p.59. Gluck, *Medallion (YouWe)*, 1936. Oil on canvas, 12 × 14 in. (30.5 × 35.6 cm). Private collection. © Gluck Estate. Photo: Courtesy The Fine Art Society Ltd.

p.60. Vanessa Bell's former studio at Charleston. © The Charleston Trust. Photo: Lee Robbins.

p.61. Vanessa Bell, book cover for Virginia Woolf's, *Three Guineas*, 1938. © Penguin Random House.

p.63. Sonia Delaunay, *Prismes électriques (Electric Prisms)*, 1914. Oil on canvas. Musée National d'Art Moderne, Centre Pompidou, Paris. © Pracusa. Photo: © 2026 Scala, Florence.

p.64. Natalia Goncharova, *Cyclist*, 1913. State Russian Museum, St. Petersburg, Russia. © UPRAVIS. Photo: Bridgeman Images.

p.65. Benedetta Cappa Marinetta, *Speeding Motorboat*, 1923–4. Galleria d'Arte Moderna, Rome. © Benedetta Cappa Marinetta, used by permission of Vittoria Marinetti and Luce Marinetti's heirs. Photo: Album/Alamy.

p.66. Hannah Höch, *Cut with the Dada Kitchen Knife through the Last Weimar Beer-Belly Cultural Epoch in Germany*, 1919. Nationalgalerie, Staatliche Museen zu Berlin. © 2025 DACS. Photo: © 2026 Scala, Florence/bpk, Berlin.

p.67 (top). Käthe Kollwitz, *The Mothers*, sheet 6 of the series War, 1922. Woodcut, 13.39 × 15.75 in. (34 × 40 cm). Kn 176 VII b. Käthe Kollwitz Museum Köln, Inv. No. 70300/92016, www.kollwitz.de.

p.67 (bottom). Jeanne (Gertrud) Mammen, *She Represents*, c. 1928. Private collection. © 2025 DACS. Photo: akg-images.

p.70 (top). Leonor Fini at a masked ball, Venice, 1953. Photo: Archivio Cameraphoto Epoche/Getty Images

p.70 (bottom). Leonor Fini, *La Passagère (The Passenger)*, 1964. Cat. 683, page 409, ref. no. 0703. © 2025 ADAGP, Paris and DACS, London. Photo: Courtesy Galerie Minsky, Paris.

p.71. Ithell Colquhoun, *Scylla*, 1938. Tate, London. © Noise Abatement Society, © Samaritans, © Spire Healthcare.

p.72. Leonora Carrington, Portrait of *Max Ernst*, 1939. © 2025 Estate of Leonora Carrington/ARS, NY and DACS, London. Photo: photosublime/Alamy.

p.73 (top). Gertrude Abercrombie, *Three Cats*, 1956. Private collection. Photo: Courtesy of Freeman's/Hindman.

p.73 (bottom). Lee Miller, *Surgical Gloves are sterilised and dried on stands, Churchill Hospital, Oxford, England*, 1943 (*4834-111*). © Lee Miller Archives, England 2025. All rights reserved www.leemiller.co.uk.

p.75 (top). Frida Kahlo, *Diego and I*, 1949. Private Collection. Photo: Fine Art Images/Bridgeman Images.

p.75 (centre). Frida Kahlo, *The Two Fridas*, 1939. Museo de Arte Moderno, Mexico City. Photo: Luisa Ricciarini/Bridgeman Images.

p.75 (bottom). Frida Kahlo, *Self-Portrait with Thorn Necklace and Hummingbird*, 1940. Harry Ransom Center, University of Texas at Austin, Austin. Photo: Bridgeman Images.

p.78 (top). Meta Vaux Warrick Fuller, *Ethiopia*, c. 1921. Paint on plaster, 13 × 3.5 × 3.88 in. (33 × 8.9 × 9.8 cm). Collection of the Smithsonian National Museum of African American History and Culture, Gift of the Fuller Family (2013.242.1) © Meta Vaux Warrick Fuller. Photo: NMAAHC.

p.78 (bottom). Augusta Savage, *Gwendolyn Knight*, 1934–5. Bronze, 17.31 × 8.5 × 8 in. (44 × 21.6 × 20.3 cm). Telfair Museum of Art, Savannah. Georgia; Gift of Walter and Linda Evans.

p.79. Augusta Savage, *Lift Every Voice and Sing (The Harp)*, 1939. Installation view, New York World's Fair. Photo: Sherman Oaks Antique Mall/Getty Images.

p.80. Selma Burke with her portrait of President Franklin D. Roosevelt, 1945. John W. Mosley Photograph Collection, Charles L. Blockson Afro-American Collection, Temple University Libraries, Philadelphia.

p.81 (left). Lois Mailou Jones, *Les Fétiches*, 1938. Smithsonian American Nan Art Museum, Washington, D.C. Museum purchase made possible by Mrs. Norvin H. Green, Dr. R. Harlan, and Francis Musgrave. Photo: © Smithsonian American Art Museum/Art Resource/Scala, Florence.

p.81 (right). Marc Vaux, *Lois Mailou Jones painting in her studio with her cat*, c.1937–8. © Centre Pompidou-MNAM/CCI-Bibliothèque Kandinsky, Paris. Fonds Marc Vaux, MV 8421. Photo: RMN-Grand Palais/Fonds Marc Vaux/Scala, Florence.

p.84. Tarsila do Amaral, *Morro da Favela (Favella Hill)*, 1924. Hecilda and Sergio Fadel Collection, Rio de Janeiro. Photo: Jaime Acioli © Tarsila do Amaral Licenciamentos.

p.85. Tarsila do Amaral, *Carnaval Em Madureira (Carnival in Madureira)*, 1924. Pinacoteca do Estado, São Paulo. © Tarsila do Amaral Licenciamentos.

p.86. Georgia O'Keeffe, *Radiator Building–Night, New York*, 1927. Alfred Stieglitz Collection, Co-owned by Fisk University, Nashville, Tennessee, and Crystal Bridges Museum of American Art, Bentonville, Arkansas. © Georgia O'Keeffe Museum/ DACS 2025. Photo: Edward C. Robison III.

p.87. Georgia O'Keeffe, *Black Mesa Landscape, New Mexico (Out Back of Marie's II)*, 1930. Oil on canvas mounted to board. Georgia O'Keeffe Museum, Santa Fe. Burnett Foundation Gift. © Georgia O'Keeffe Museum/DACS 2025. Photo: © Georgia O'Keeffe Museum/Art Resource, NY/Scala, Florence.

p.90–1. Lee Krasner, *The Seasons*, 1957. Oil and house paint on canvas, overall: 92.75 × 203.88 in. (235.6 × 517.8 cm). Whitney Museum of American Art, New York. Purchase, with funds from Frances and Sydney Lewis by exchange, the Mrs. Percy Uris Purchase Fund and the Painting and Sculpture Committee. © 2025 The Pollock-Krasner Foundation/ ARS, NY and DACS, London. Photo: Whitney Museum of American Art/Licensed by Scala.

p.92. Joan Mitchell, *Weeds*, 1976. Oil on canvas, 110.5 × 157.5 in. (280.7 × 400.1 cm). Hirshhorn Museum and Sculpture Garden, Washington, D.C. © Estate of Joan Mitchell.

p.93. Joan Mitchell, *Daylight*, c.1975. Pastel and typewriter ink on paper, 14 × 9 in. (35.6 × 22.9 cm). Private collection. © Estate of Joan Mitchell, New York. Incorporating poem Daylight by James Schuyler, 1974. © by permission of Farrar Straus & Giroux.

p.96. Atsuko Tanaka wearing her *Electric Dress* suspended from the temporary beam at the 2nd Gutai Art Exhibition in Ohara Hall, Tokyo, 1956. © Kanayama Akira and Tanaka Atsuko Association.

p.97. Anni Albers, *Black-White-Yellow*, Original 1926 (lost), re-woven by Gunta Stölzl, 1965. Mercerized cotton, silk, 80 × 47.5 in. (203.2 × 120.7 cm). Metropolitan Museum of Art, New York. Purchase, Everfast Fabrics Inc. and Edward C. Moore Jr. Gift, 1969. © 2026 The Josef and Anni Albers Foundation/Artists Rights Society (ARS) New York/DACS, London. Photo: © 2026 Met, NY/Art Resource/Scala, Florence.

p.98. Installation view of Ruth Asawa: *Life's Work* at the Pulitzer Arts Foundation, St Louis, Missouri, September 14, 2018 – February 16, 2019. © Estate of Ruth Asawa. Courtesy The Estate of Ruth Asawa and David Zwirner. Photograph © Alise O'Brien Photography.

p.101. Yayoi Kusama, *Infinity Nets* (1), 1958. Oil on canvas, 125.3 × 91 cm. © YAYOI KUSAMA. Courtesy of Ota Fine Arts.

p.102 (top). Yayoi Kusama at work, 2013. Photo by Gautier Deblonde. Artwork © YAYOI KUSAMA. Courtesy of Ota Fine Arts.

p.102 (bottom). Yayoi Kusama, *Pumpkin*, 1994, restored 2022. Naoshima, Kagawa Prefecture. Reproduced with permission of Benesse Art Site. © YAYOI KUSAMA. Courtesy of Ota Fine Arts. Photo: Kat Davis/Alamy.

p.103 (top). Yayoi Kusama, *Infinity Mirrored Room – The Souls of Millions of Light Years Away*, 2013. 415.0 × 415.0 × 287.7cm. Mixed media. © YAYOI KUSAMA.

p.103 (bottom). Photograph of Yayoi Kusama by Yusuke Miyazaki. Courtesy Ota Fine Arts, David Zwirner and Victoria Miro. © YAYOI KUSAMA.p.104. Alma Thomas, *Blast Off*, 1970. Acrylic on canvas. Smithsonian National Air and Space Museum. Gift of Vincent Melzac.

p.105 (top). Bridget Riley, *Gala*, 1974. Acrylic on canvas, 62.75 × 62.75 in. (159.5 × 159.5 cm). © Bridget Riley 2025. All rights reserved.

p.105 (bottom). Etel Adnan, *Untitled*, 2014. Oil on canvas, 13.75 × 10.63 in. (35 × 27cm). © Succession Etel Adnan. Photo: © White Cube/George Darrell.

p.107. Sister Mary Corita (Corita Kent), *enriched bread*, 1965. Serigraph, courtesy of Corita Art Center, corita.org. © Courtesy of the Corita Art Center, Immaculate Heart Community, Los Angeles© 2025 ARS, NY and DACS, London.

p.108. Pauline Boty, *The Only Blonde in the World*, 1963. Tate Gallery, London. Courtesy of the Pauline Boty Estate.

p.109. Evelyne Axell, *Ice Cream 1*, 1964. Collection of Serge Goisse, Belgium. © 2025 ADAGP, Paris and DACS, London. Photo: Paul Louis.

p.110. Evelyne Axell, *Valentine*, 1966. Tate Gallery, London. © ADAGP, Paris and DACS, London 2026. Photo: Paul Louis.

p.111 (top). Advertisement for Wayenberg Massagic shoes, 1972.

p.111 (bottom). Marisol, *Dinner Date*, 1963. Painted wood, plaster, textiles, oil on canvas, metal fork, leather boots, paint, graphite, 55 × 53.5 × 44 in. (139.7 × 135.9 × 111.8 cm). Yale University Art Gallery, New Haven. Gift of Susan Morse Hilles (1973.86). © 2025 Estate of Marisol/ ARS, New York & DACS, London.

p.114 (left and right). Elizabeth Catlett, *Black Unity*, 1968. Cedar, 21 × 12.5 × 23 in. (53.34 × 31.75 × 58.42 cm). Crystal Bridges Museum of American Art, Bentonville, Arkansas, 2014.11. Photography by Edward C. Robison III. © 2025 Catlett Mora Family Trust/VAGA at ARS, NY and DACS, London

p.115. Tommie Smith and John Carlos raise the Black Power salute. Olympic Games, Mexico City, 1968. Photo: Getty Images.

p.116. Barbara Jones-Hogu, *Unite*, 1971. Screen print, 22.5 × 30 in. (57.15 × 76.2 cm). Art Institute of Chicago. Gift of Judy and Patrick Diamond. © Estate of Barbara Jones-Hogu. Photo: Bridgeman Images.

p.117. Carolyn Mims Lawrence, *Black Children Keep Your Spirits Free*, 1972. Acrylic on canvas, 49 × 51 × 2 in. (124.5 × 129.5 × 5.1 cm). © Carolyn Mims Lawrence. Photo: Michael Tropea.

p.119, Faith Ringgold, *American People*, 2022. Exhibition view. New Museum, New York. Photo: Dario Lasagni. Courtesy New Museum. © Faith Ringgold / ARS, NY and DACS, London, courtesy ACA Galleries, New York 2022.

p.122 (top). Sheila Hicks, *Pillar of Inquiry/Supple Column*, 2013–4. Installation view, Whitney Museum of American Art, New York. Photo: Bill Orcutt/Licensed by Scala. © Sheila Hicks.

p.122 (bottom). Sheila Hicks pictured during *Foray into Chromatic Zones*, 2015. Hayward Gallery Project Space, Southbank, London. Artwork: © Sheila Hicks. Photo: Guy Bell/Alamy.

p.123 (top). Mrinalini Mukherjee with her work, *PRITHVI (Woman on a Swing)*, 1989. Hemp, 100.39 × 38.98 × 27.56 in. (255 × 99 × 70 cm). © Mrinalini Mukherjee Foundation.

p.123 (centre). Inca quipu, c.1400–1532. Brooklyn Museum, New York, Gift of Ernest Erickson, 70.177.69. Creative Commons Attribution 3.0 (Generic).

p.123 (bottom). Cecilia Vicuña, *Quipu Womb (The Story of the Red Thread, Athens)*, 2017. Unspun wool, dyed, 236.22 × 314.96 in. (600 × 800 cm). Installation view, documenta 14, EMST – National Museum of Contemporary Art, Athens, Greece, 2017. Courtesy the artist and Lehmann Maupin, New York, Seoul, and London. © 2025 Cecilia Vicuña/ARS, NY and DACS, London. Photo: Mathias Voelzke.

p.124. Judith Scott, *Untitled*, 1997. Fiber and found objects, 17.5 × 75 × 21 in. (44.45 × 109.5 × 53.34 cm). (JS 70). Courtesy of the artist and Creative Growth.

p.125. Loretta Pettway Bennett, *Work-clothes strips*, 2003. Demin, 79 × 60 in. (200.7 × 152.4 cm). Courtesy Souls Grown Deep Foundation and Alison Jacques © 2025 Loretta Pettway Bennett/ ARS, NY and DACS, London.

p.129 (left). Judy Chicago, Virginia Woolf place setting from *The Dinner Party*, 1974–1979. Mixed media. Collection of Brooklyn Museum, gift of the Elizabeth A. Sackler Foundation. © 2025 Chicago Woodman LLC, Judy Chicago/ DACS. Photo: © Chicago Woodman LLC, Donald Woodman/DACS.

p.129 (right). Judy Chicago, *The Dinner Party*, 1974–9. Ceramic, porcelain, textile, 576 × 576 in. (1463 × 1463 cm). Brooklyn Museum, Gift of the Elizabeth A. Sackler Foundation, 2002.10. © 2025 Chicago Woodman LLC, Judy Chicago/ DACS. Photo: © Chicago Woodman LLC, Donald Woodman/DACS.

p.130 (top). Faith Ringgold, *Woman Freedom Now*, 1971. Offset print, 28.5 × 19 in. (72.39 × 48.26 cm). © 2025 Anyone Can Fly Foundation/DACS.

p.130 (bottom). Faith Ringgold, *For the Women's House*, 1971. Oil on canvas, 96 × 96 in. (243.84 × 243.84 cm). © 2025 Anyone Can Fly Foundation/DACS. Image courtesy of the artist and Rose M. Singer Center, New York.

p.131 (left). Alice Neel, *Linda Nochlin and Daisy*, 1973. Oil on canvas, 55.87 × 44.2 in. (141.9 × 111.8 cm). © The Estate of Alice Neel. Courtesy The Estate of Alice Neel and David Zwirner.

p.131 (right). Alice Neel, *Benjamin*, 1976. Acrylic on board, 29.88 × 20.75 in. (75.9 × 52.7 cm). © The Estate of Alice Neel. Courtesy The Estate of Alice Neel and David Zwirner.

p.133 (top). Guerrilla Girls, *How Many Women Had One-Person Exhibitions at NYC Museums Last Year?*, 1985. © Guerrilla Girls, courtesy guerrillagirls.com.

p.133 (bottom). Guerrilla Girls, *The Advantages of Being a Woman Artist*, 1988. © Guerrilla Girls, courtesy guerrillagirls.com.

p.134 (top). Cindy Sherman, *Untitled Film Still #10*, 1978. Gelatin silver print, 8 × 10 in. (20.32 × 25.4 cm). © Cindy Sherman. Courtesy the artist and Hauser & Wirth.

p.134 (bottom). Cindy Sherman, *Untitled Film Still #56*, 1980. Gelatin silver print, 8 × 10 in. (20.32 × 25.4 cm). © Cindy Sherman. Courtesy the artist and Hauser & Wirth.

p.135 (right). Cindy Sherman, Untitled, 2003. Chromogenic color print. © Cindy Sherman. Courtesy the artist and Hauser & Wirth.

p.136. Agnes Denes, Wheatfield – A Confrontation: *Battery Park Landfill, Downtown Manhattan – With Statue of Liberty Across the Hudson*, 1982. © Agnes Denes, Courtesy Leslie Tonkonow Artworks + Projects.

p.137. Agnes Denes, *Wheatfield – A Confrontation: Battery Park Landfill, Downtown Manhattan – With New York Financial Center*, 1982. © Agnes Denes, Courtesy Leslie Tonkonow Artworks + Projects.

p.138. Lorraine O'Grady, *Art Is... (Troupe with Mlle Bourgeoise Noire)*, 1983/2009. C-print in 40 parts, 16 × 20 in. (40.64 × 50.8 cm). Edition of 8 + 1 AP. Courtesy Mariane Ibrahim Gallery. © 2025 Lorraine O'Grady Trust/ DACS.

p.138 (top). Lorraine O'Grady, *Art Is... (Dancer in a Grass Skirt)*, 1983/2009. C-print in 40 parts, 16 × 20 in. (40.64 × 50.8 cm). Edition of 8 + 1 AP. Courtesy Mariane Ibrahim Gallery. © 2025 Lorraine O'Grady Trust/DACS.

p.138 (bottom). Lorraine O'Grady, *Art Is... (Girlfriends Times Two)*, 1983/2009. C-print in 40 parts. 16 × 20 in. (40.64 × 50.8 cm). Edition of 8 + 1 AP. Courtesy Mariane Ibrahim Gallery. © 2025 Lorraine O'Grady Trust/ DACS.

p.142. Tracey Emin, *My Bed*, 1998. Courtesy Saatchi Gallery, London. © 2025 Tracey Emin. All rights reserved, DACS. Photo: Prudence Cuming Associates Ltd.

p.143. Rachel Whiteread, *House*, 1993 (destroyed 1994). Concrete, wood and steel. Commissioned by Artangel. Sponsored by Beck's. © Rachel Whiteread.

p.144. Cornelia Parker, *Cold Dark Matter: An Exploded View*, 1991. Installation view: Tate Britain, 19 May–16 October 2022. Wood, metal, plastic, ceramic, paper, textile and wire. © Cornelia Parker. Photo: © Tate.

p.145 (left). Gillian Wearing, *Signs that say what you want them to say and not Signs that say what someone else wants you to say BEST FRIENDS FOR LIFE! LONG LIVE THE TWO OF US.*, 1992–3. C-type print on aluminium, 17.51 × 11.69 in. (44.5 × 29.7 cm). © Gillian Wearing, courtesy Maureen Paley, London, Tanya Bonakdar Gallery, New York and Regen Projects, Los Angeles.

p.145 (right). Gillian Wearing, Signs that say what you want them to say and not Signs that say what someone else wants you to say *I'M DESPERATE*, 1992–3. C-type print on aluminium, 17.51 × 11.69 in. (44.5 × 29.7 cm). © Gillian Wearing, courtesy Maureen Paley, London, Tanya Bonakdar Gallery, New York and Regen Projects, Los Angeles.

p.147. Alma Nungarrayi Granites, *Napaljarri-Warnu Jukurrpa (Star or Seven Sisters Dreaming)*, 2011. © 2025 Alma Nungarrayi Granites/Copyright Agency. Licensed by DACS

p.148. Tjungkara Ken, Sandra Ken, Yaritji Young, Freda Brady and Maringka Tunkin, Pitjantjatjara people, *Seven Sisters*, 2018. National Gallery of Australia, Canberra purchased 2020. © 2025 Tjunkara Ken, Sandra Ken, Yaritji Young, Freda Brady, Maringka Tunkin/Copyright Agency. Licensed by DACS.

p.149. Kathleen Ngal, Anmatyerre people, *Untitled*, 2010. Synthetic polymer paint on canvas, 72.44 × 119.88 in. (184 × 304.5cm). Queensland Art Gallery, Gallery of Modern Art, Brisbane. Gift of Donald Holt through the Queensland Art Gallery Foundation 2013 © Kathleen Ngala/Copyright Agency. Licensed by DACS.

p.150–1. Emily Kam Kngwarreye, Anmatyerre people, *Yam awely*, 1995. Synthetic polymer paint on canvas. National Gallery of Australia, Canberra. Gift of the Delmore Collection, Donald and Janet Holt 1995. © 2025 Emily Kam Kngwarray/Copyright Agency. Licensed by DACS.

p.151 (bottom). Kitty Kantilla, *Purrukuparli* (left) and *Wai-ai* (right), 1995. National Gallery of Victoria, Melbourne. Presented through The Art Foundation of Victoria with the assistance of The Peter and Susan Rowland Endowment, Governor, 1995 © 2025 Kitty Kantilla / Copyright Agency. Licensed by DACS.

p.153 (left). Tate Modern Turbine Hall before refurbishment. Photo: © Tate.

p.153 (right). Doris Salcedo, *Shibboleth II*, from *Shibboleth*, 2007. Crack in the floor of Tate Modern Turbine Hall. Installation, 9 October 2007–24 March 2008. © Doris Salcedo. Photo: © Tate.

p.153 (bottom). Rachel Whiteread, Embankment, 2005. Installation view for *The Unilever Series: Rachel Whiteread, Embankment*, October 2005–May 2006, Turbine Hall, Tate Modern, London. © Rachel Whiteread. Photo: © Tate.

p.154. Louise Bourgeois, Maman, 1999. Installation photo, *The Unilever Series: Louise Bourgeois, I Do, I Undo and I Redo*, May–December 2000, Turbine Hall, Tate Modern. © 2025 The Easton Foundation/VAGA at ARS, NY and DACS, London. Photo: Marcus Leith and Andrew Dunkley © Tate Photography.

p.156. Victoria Memorial, The Mall, London, by Thomas Brock. Photo: Shutterstock.

p.157. Kara Walker, *Fons Americanus*, 2019. Non-toxic acrylic and cement composite, recyclable cork, wood, and metal. Main: 73.5 × 50 × 43 feet (22.4 × 15.2 × 13.2 meters); Grotto: 10.2 × 10.5 × 10.8 feet (3.1 × 3.2 × 3.3 meters). Installation view: Hyundai Commission: Kara Walker – Fons Americanus, Tate Modern, London, UK, 2019 © Kara Walker, courtesy of Sikkema Malloy Jenkins and Sprüth Magers. Photo: © Tate/Matt Greenwood.

p.159 (top). Sarah Sze, *Metronome*, 2023. Mixed media, projectors, paper, wood, stainless steel. Installation, ARoS Aarhus Kunstmuseum, 2024. © Sarah Sze. Photo: Andrea Rosetti.

p.159 (bottom). Julie Mehretu, *Empirical Construction, Istanbul*, 2003. Acrylic and ink on canvas, 10 × 15 in. (304.8 × 457.2 cm). MoMA, New York. Fund for the Twenty-First Century (323.2004). © 2025 Julie Mehretu. Photo: Digital image, The Museum of Modern Art, New York/Scala, Florence.

p.160. Lavinia Fontana, *Bianca degli Utili Maselli with six of her children*, c.1604–5. Fine Arts Museums of San Francisco. Photo: Sotheby's/Alamy.

p.161 (top). Carrie Mae Weems, *Untitled (Woman and daughter with makeup)*, 1990. Archival pigment print, 40 × 40 in. (101.6 × 101.6 cm). © Carrie Mae Weems. Courtesy the artist and Gladstone Gallery, New York.

p.161 (bottom). Mickalene Thomas, *Le Dejeuner sur l'herbe: Les trois femmes noires*, 2010. Rhinestones, acrylic, and enamel on wood panel, 120 × 288 in. (304.8 × 731.5 cm). The Rachel and Jean-Pierre Lehmann Collection. © 2025 Mickalene Thomas/ARS, NY and DACS, London.

p.162 (top). Chantal Joffe, *Katy in a Yellow Suit*, 2023. Oil on canvas, 82.75 × 41.36 in. (210.3 × 105 cm). © Chantal Joffe. Courtesy the artist and Victoria Miro. Photo: Jack Hems.

p.162 (bottom left). Chantal Joffe, *Self-Portrait with Esme*, 2009. Oil on linen. 84.13 × 60.13 × 1.25 in. (213.5 × 152.5 × 3.3 cm). © Chantal Joffe. Courtesy the artist and Victoria Miro. Photo: Stephen White & Co.

p.162 (bottom centre). Chantal Joffe, *Poppy, Esme, Oleanna, Gracie and Kate*, 2014. Oil on canvas, 15.75 × 31.5 in. (40 × 80 cm). © Chantal Joffe. Courtesy the artist and Victoria Miro. Photo: Stephen White & Co.

p.162 (bottom right). Chantal Joffe, *Prom*, 2022. Oil on panel, 110.25 × 79.86 in. (280 × 203 cm). © Chantal Joffe. Courtesy the artist and Victoria Miro. Photo: Jack Hems.

p.163 (top). Zanele Muholi, *Bester I, Mayotte*, 2015. © Zanele Muholi. Courtesy of the artist and Yancey Richardson, New York.

p.163 (bottom right). Harry Weller, Tracey Emin with *The Doors*, 2023. Artwork: © 2025 Tracey Emin. All rights reserved, DACS. Photo: © Harry Weller.

p.165. Flora Yukhnovich, *She is Beauty and She is Grace*, 2022. Oil on linen. Overall dimensions 240 × 474 cm (94 ½ x 186 5/8 in.). © Flora Yukhnovich. Courtesy the artist, Hauser & Wirth and Victoria Miro.

ACKNOWLEDGEMENTS

There are so many wonderful people who help make books possible, especially this one. Thank you to my brilliant editors, Tom Rawlinson and Phoebe Jascourt, and their excellent wider team: Sarah Connelly, Andrea Kearney, Ella Thomson, Sophie Gordon, Cecilia Mackay, Caroline Curtis, Lucy Doncaster, Pippa Shaw, Corinne Lucas, Lauren Floodgate and Daisy Northway. Thank you to my whizz of an agent, Karolina Sutton, her assistant Izzy Redfern, and the team at CAA. Thank you to the Cornerstone team, who make my adult books a reality, and a special thanks to Ping Zhu, whose illustrations light up this book!

Thank you to all the artists and artists' estates included in this book, who gave me permission to feature your words and works, and to the experts who very kindly fact-checked sections: Maria H. Loh, Ena Morita, Christopher Adams, Deirdre Maher and Cindy Kang (and the Barnes Foundation), Eric Gleason, Jenny Gill and Laura Morris (and the Joan Mitchell Foundation), Lisa Warring, Wendi Norris, Anya Udovik, Tina Baum, Erin Vink, Beatrice Gralton, Agnes Denes, Sheila Barker, Patrick Duffy, Martha Greenhough, Masami Yamada, Mary Redfern, Sara Chan, Harry Weller, Tracey Emin, Joanna Moorhead, Megan Schultz and Judy Chicago, Julie Niemi, Annabelle Birchenough, Ali MacGilp, Ami Bouhassane, Maggie Wright, Lauren Williamson, Luis Martin Lozano, Georgia Gardner, Jessica Simas, Cortney Norman, Martin Coppell, Fiona Amitai, Alison Jacques, Isabel Mackenzie, Rebecca Lyons and Annette Wickham, Ming Tiampo, Bridget R Cooks, Jennifer M. Swope, Sonal Khullar, Nina Cahill, Magdalene Keaney, Emma Mckee, Christine McMonagle, Catherine Morris, Matthew Tom, Amelia Peck, Julia Voss, Eve O'Brien and Grace Hong, Connor Monahan, Alex O'Neill and Emma Vooght, Rebecca Bray, Annabell Potter, Claire Pauley McPherson, Melanie Herzog, Darren Clarke, Wanda M. Corn, Sue Tate, Amy Lim, Nellie Scott, Alice Sebrell, Chloe Staid, Chantal Joffe, Bea Bradley and Erin Manns.

Thank you to my brilliant assistant, Molly LaFosse; Gilda Williams for your eagle eye; Violet and Lucas for coming around museums with me; Holly Bott and Kate Cooper, and of course to my wonderful friends and family: Mum, Dad, Sarah, Felix, Michael, Katie, Victoria, Louisa (Jesse, Phoebe, Thea, Cleo).